What to Expect for First Time Moms and Pregnancy Secrets

The Complete Stress-Free Guide While Expecting, Discover Leading Recommendations for The First Year, A Healthy Newborn and Childbirth

Catherine Emily

© **Copyright 2019 - All rights reserved.**

The content contained within this book may not be reproduced, duplicated or transmitted without direct written permission from the author or the publisher.

Under no circumstances will any blame or legal responsibility be held against the publisher, or author, for any damages, reparation, or monetary loss due to the information contained within this book. Either directly or indirectly.

Legal Notice

This book is copyright protected. This book is only for personal use. You cannot amend, distribute, sell, use, quote or paraphrase any part, or the content within this book, without the consent of the author or publisher.

Disclaimer Notice

Please note the information contained within this document is for educational and entertainment purposes only. All effort has been executed to present accurate, up to date, and reliable, complete information. No warranties of any kind are declared or implied. Readers acknowledge that the author is not engaging in the rendering of legal, financial, medical or professinnal advice. The content within this book has been derived from various sources. Please consult a licensed professional before attempting any techniques outlined in this book.

By reading this document, the reader agrees that under no circumstances is the author responsible for any losses, direct or indirect, which are incurred as a result of the use of information contained within this document, including, but not limited to, — errors, omissions, or inaccuracies.

Contents

Expecting First Time Moms 1

Chapter 1:
The Start of Your 9-Month Journey 2

Chapter 2:
Selecting Your OB/GYN..10

Chapter 3:
The Morning Sickness Remedy 20

Chapter 4:
Exercising Do's and Don'ts 30

Chapter 5:
Sleeping the Right Way 37

Chapter 6:
Nutrition and Top Foods to Eat...45

Chapter 7:
Tips to Curb Cravings 54

Chapter 8:
The First Trimester, Weeks 1 to 12 60

Chapter 9:
The Second Trimester, Weeks 13 to 26 66

Chapter 10:
The Third Trimester, Weeks 27 to 40 72

Chapter 11:
The Stages of Labor 80

Chapter 12:
Hypnobirthing 89

Chapter 13:
Post-Partum Recovery 98

Chapter 14:
Detrimental Mistakes to Avoid During Pregnancy 108

Chapter 15:
Top Pregnancy Tips and Essentials 119

Mindful Pregnancy for New Moms 132

Chapter 1:
Things I Wish I Knew While Pregnant 133

Chapter 2:
Get Your Pregnancy Off to A Good Start 139

Chapter 3:
Morning Sickness No More 150

Chapter 4:
Nutrition and Food (Must Know Secrets)...156

Chapter 5:
Approved Exercises..176

Chapter 6:
Money Saving Hacks for Maternity Clothing 184

Chapter 7:
First Trimester Essential Secrets..190

Chapter 8:
Second Trimester Essential Secrets...199

Chapter 9:
Third Trimester Essential Secrets..215

Chapter 10:
Prevent Stretch Marks Hacks..226

Chapter 11:
Necessity Bag Items to Bring for Labor 232

Chapter 12:
Essential Recovery Secrets After Birth 242

Chapter 13:
Losing the Weight After Birth 249

Chapter 14:
Newborn Must Haves 258

Chapter 15:
Don't Fall for These Money Traps 267

2 IN 1 VALUE

WHAT TO EXPECT FOR

FIRST TIME MOMS
AND
PREGNANCY SECRETS

The Complete Stress Free Guide While Expecting, Discover Leading Recommendations for The First Year, A Healthy Newborn and Childbirth

CATHERINE EMILY

Expecting First Time Moms

The Complete Day by Day Pregnancy Guide on What You Should Expect for a Healthy First Year, Motherhood, Childbirth, and Newborn from Leading Experts who Are Parents too

Catherine Emily

Chapter 1:
The Start of Your 9-Month Journey

It has been said there are events in a lifetime that are so significant that they leave a distinct 'before' and 'after' in your life and in you as a person. The day you find out that you are expecting your first child is one such event. The feelings that a woman experiences when that pregnancy test turns positive can only be felt and understood by the woman herself. In the case of an unexpected pregnancy, there might be shock and panic. In the case of a long-awaited child, joy and happiness can be overwhelming and leave you in tears. Apprehension, anxiety, and fear are some of the other feelings a woman might experience after finding out that they are going to be a mother. After these emotions settle, you are likely going to experience an overwhelming urge to start planning. Some women will start buying baby clothes immediately after finding out that they are pregnant.

Usually, a woman suspects that they are pregnant even before they take that pregnancy test. This suspicion could be because of the way they feel or because of the circumstances of the previous weeks. The best way to be sure is to take a pregnancy test. A positive pregnancy test can be confirmed at the hospital, at which point you'll know for sure that there's no turning back. Questioning whether you're up to the task of being a mother is a common and natural emotion to experience after finding out that you are pregnant. Are you ready? Is your partner ready? Is your career ready? These are just some everyday worries that women go through. It is essential that you prioritize having a safe and healthy pregnancy above anything else that can be handled later.

There is no 'perfect' approach to pregnancy, but there are certain guidelines that are generally accepted as requirements for a healthy pregnancy and childbirth. For starters, after finding out that you are pregnant, you'll need to kick all your bad habits to the curb. Smoking and excessive consumption of alcohol are two examples of things you'll need to forget. Some things that are not exactly textbook-bad will need to go too. For instance, if you have previously enjoyed sushi, you'll have to make do without it for the next nine months. If you enjoyed contact sports before you got pregnant, you might want to settle for yoga instead. If you were a fan of long, hot baths, you might need to settle for showers instead. In short, pregnancy will change your life. You must be ready for these changes.

Being ready will incorporate the physical and the mental. It is often said that your attitude can change the course of your life, and this is true for pregnancy. A positive attitude during pregnancy will make this journey more enjoyable and memorable for the right reasons. Thanks to all the hormonal changes that occur during pregnancy, you're likely to experience mild to severe mood swings which can throw quite the spanner into the works. Stay conscious of your emotions and keep a positive mindset. Meditation, taking a relaxing bath, having an honest, open conversation with a confidant, and therapy can help you manage all the differing emotions that you'll experience during this period. Staying mentally and physically healthy during pregnancy will increase your chances of remaining healthy and happy after becoming a mom.

Just like some girls plan their dream wedding well in advance, some moms plan their kids' births even before they get pregnant. Whether you're the type that likes to start early or the kind that prefers to arrive late, it is important that you at least have a rough plan in mind. Over the coming months, you can refine your plan to include more details. A significant decision you'll need to make is whether you wish to have a home birth or hospital birth. If you wish to have a home birth, you'll need to choose a good midwife and a doula who will assist you with the delivery.

A midwife is a health care provider who can deliver babies, while a doula is more of a professional support system for you. A doula will teach you how to manage the pain of childbirth including guiding you on breathing techniques. A good midwife and a good doula are vital assets to have during delivery. On the flipside, if you opt to go to the hospital, you'll need to start looking for a good hospital and preferably one that accepts your insurance plan, if you have one. It is important to note that a midwife can also help you deliver at a hospital.

Throughout the next nine months, your baby will grow from the size of an orange seed to the size of a small pumpkin or watermelon. You will experience hormonal, physical, and emotional changes as your baby grows. Some of these changes will be wonderful, and others will be unpleasant. Keeping your eye on the goal will take you through the most challenging days. Learning how to manage the manageable changes will come in handy — worried about stretch marks? Get yourself a sweet moisturizing cream like cocoa buttercream to keep your skin soft and stretchy, so it's not pulled too tight. Take care of your skin by paying attention to what you put inside of your body. Fruits like oranges that are packed with vitamin C are recommended. Some things will be mostly outside of your control as far as managing them goes. Are you worried about gaining weight? You do not have a whole lot of choice in this when you are growing a baby inside of you. You need to ensure that you're eating the right things.

Your womanhood should not take a backseat during pregnancy. Pregnancy is a time to celebrate not just the baby inside of you but you as a woman as well. A lot of times, pregnant women forget to take care of themselves and focus a lot on nurturing the pregnancy. It is advisable and vital that you make time to do the things you enjoy as a woman and as a person. This self-care should continue even after the baby arrives. Pamper yourself by going for pedicures and manicures and allow others to pamper you when they want to. As far as going to the spa is concerned, check with your doctor first as specific spa treatments could harm your baby. For instance, it is generally advised to hold off massages and intensive facials until you're into your second trimester. Saunas are a no-no for the entire duration of your pregnancy, as they can cause overheating which is dangerous to the baby.

Dental care is another form of self-care that you'll need to observe during your pregnancy. You might probably have heard it said that dentists are not too keen to offer dental treatments to pregnant women. This is not entirely true. Dental work that is necessary and urgent such as treatment of a cavity can be carried out during pregnancy. For dental work that is mainly aesthetic, such as teeth whitening, it is usually best to wait until after delivery. While pregnant, your dentist will use the minimum dose of anesthesia and will likely recommend that you visit during your second trimester. In your third trimester, you are likely to be very uncomfortable lying on your back in the dentist's chair.

A good health insurance plan will alleviate your financial worries during your pregnancy. Good healthcare is not exactly cheap and knowing that your insurance provider is carrying the more massive load of the financial burden will mean one less problem on your plate. Ideally, it is best to get on an insurance plan before you get pregnant. If you were not on an insurance cover before you got pregnant, you could still get the coverage you need for your maternity needs. Being uninsured could cost you tens of thousands of dollars over the next nine months, so it's always advisable to get on board an insurance cover.

While most women are more than willing to share the good news of their pregnancy with their loved ones, the tune changes when it comes to facing the employer. It can be challenging to break the news of your pregnancy to your boss, especially when you are apprehensive about how your maternity break will affect your career aspirations. It is good practice to let your employer know you are expecting and will be away from work before they find out for themselves. Sharing this information early on allows your employer enough time to plan for your absence, especially if they need to hire a replacement to hold the fort when you're away. Feel free to wait until you're twenty weeks along to break the news to your employer. Since your bump starts showing between weeks 12 and 16, you'll need to make sure nosy co-workers do not get to the boss before you. Layering and keeping the information to yourself until you are ready to let it be public knowledge should help. What this means is that you'll not announce anything on Facebook until you're prepared for everyone to know.

The people who love you are a priceless asset for you during pregnancy. They'll come through for you in ways you had never imagined. They'll cry tears of joy with you when you find out that you are pregnant. They'll plan your surprise baby shower for you and buy too many clothes for your baby. They'll hold your hair as you throw up during the first trimester and stay awake with you when you cannot sleep during the third trimester. Cherish these people and let them know how much they mean to you. It is easy to be a mean and terrible person when you are dealing with all the pregnancy hormones but do your best to resist the urge. Your partner may not understand how frustrating it is to get up a million times a night to pee, but they are also dealing with this life event as well. They're probably worried about what kind of father they'll be and if they'll live up to expectations. Be mindful of this and keep having the conversations that matter.

Encourage your partner to be a part of your pregnancy by signing up for childbirth education classes together. Your partner will come in handy during delivery when they are reciting to you all the useful tips that they learned during that Lamaze class. Often, it is easy for a father-to-be to feel left out from the pregnancy journey since the pregnancy is such an intimate time for baby and mom to bond. Going for classes, engaging in fun activities together, and reminding yourself why you got together in the first place is essential in telling your partner that you still need them, and they still matter to you. Make sure to schedule as many date nights as you can, since they'll probably become a thing of the past after the baby comes home.

Expecting First Time Moms

Pregnancy is a delicate period, and you need to be aware of warning signs that indicate that you need to get to the hospital. Things that could previously be ignored might need to be checked during pregnancy — having a suspicious rash down there? Get it checked. Are you feeling abnormally nauseous in the mornings? See a doctor. Are you worried that you have a urinary tract infection? Book that doctor's appointment. Do not self-medicate, especially not during pregnancy. Self-medication is the surest way to harm yourself and your baby.

Lastly, enjoy your pregnancy. It is a beautiful journey that will last only nine months, and once it's over, all you will have left are memories. Living each day at a time, while making the most of it, is the perfect way of going through the three trimesters. Accepting that you do not need to have everything figured out will give you peace of mind. The Universe chose you to be your baby's mother, and that is your sign that you are good enough for this most fulfilling job.

Chapter 2:
Selecting Your OB/GYN

After finding out that you are pregnant, you'll have to say goodbye to your general practitioner and say hello to a new kind of doctor: the obstetrician. An obstetrician is a doctor who specializes in obstetrics, which is the field concerned with all matter's pregnancy and childbirth. An obstetrician differs from a gynecologist in that gynecology focuses on the female reproductive systems without necessarily venturing into the childbirth and pregnancy process. In simple terms, your regular gynecologist might not be suited for your pregnancy unless they are an obstetrician as well.

As a first-time mother, it is crucial to choose an obstetrician who makes your pregnancy journey easier. A knowledgeable, experienced, and caring OB/GYN can help you navigate a pregnancy smoothly by offering the right professional guidance. In the event of a high-risk pregnancy, an obstetrician can ensure that all precautions are taken to guarantee the comfort and safety of mother and baby. This nine-month companion will play a significant role in ensuring the well-being of yourself and the bundle of joy growing inside of you.

Expecting First Time Moms

Some women will already have a preferred doctor way before they get pregnant. This is ideal and allows you to get started on the pregnancy journey with the right medical partner. If you haven't already chosen an obstetrician, it is not too late. You can still look for a great OB/GYN after you're already pregnant. Allow yourself enough time to look for the right doctor. Do not rush the process as this could negatively affect your pregnancy and birthing experience.

An excellent place to start looking is by asking your general physician or gynecologist for a recommendation. Ask them why they think the OB/GYN they are recommending would be a good match for you. An objective peer review will help you decide based on facts and not camaraderie.

Your family and friends are another resource you'll want to use for referrals. It's highly likely that a few births have happened within your social circle. Ask about those. Talk to your friends about their birthing experiences. Reach out to your aunties for referrals. If several people mention a specific doctor, investigate that one. They might be the right doctor for you.

You'll also want to leverage the power of social media and other online sites for your benefit. Thankfully, it has become relatively easy to find information online. Do your research and find out what people have to say about an OB/GYN. Reviews on social media sites and online forums should be taken into consideration. Remember, one bad review might be an outlier. However, if everyone seems to have had a bad experience with a certain OB/GYN, yours will not be any different.

When selecting an obstetrician, you'll need to consider your preferences. For instance, some women feel more comfortable having female doctors. Others might prefer male doctors. Start by deciding which gender you are most comfortable with. Professional experience and qualifications should always take precedence over gender.

If you wish to avoid out of pocket costs, go for obstetricians that are recommended through your insurance coverage. Your insurance provider will provide a list of physicians and hospitals covered by your plan. If you do not already have this list, you can request one. This list will also help you choose a doctor who has access to your preferred hospital if you already have one. If you are not tied down by the restrictions of an insurer, you have more leeway when it comes to choosing hospitals and doctors especially if you have an unlimited budget.

Consider the accessibility of the obstetrician, in terms of physical distance and after-hours policy. You'll want to choose a doctor you can easily reach should you need to. You really do not want to be driving for hours to get to your OB/GYN's office, as this could be extremely exhausting especially in the last weeks of your pregnancy. As far as after-hours are concerned, choose an OB/GYN who is available to take care of you in times of emergencies. Emergencies do not always wait for working hours, and you need someone you can always reach.

At the very least, choose an obstetrician who has a back-up plan if they are unreachable. If you opt for a group practice, ensure you are aware of who should take over when your usual OB/GYN is away. If it is a private practice, ask about the arrangements that have been made to take care of patients when the sole doctor is not on call.

Consider making a list of three doctors who meet your preliminary criteria (whatever this might be) and arrange for a meeting with each of them. This meeting will be your chance to ask important questions and determine if you are comfortable around them. Remember, a doctor might be highly experienced and still not be a good fit for you. For your pregnancy and birthing experience, you need someone with whom you fit well, someone that you are genuinely and wholesomely comfortable around, as there will be lots of bare-naked truths to share during this journey.

Some of the questions you can ask during the first meet and greet session with your obstetrician include:

- How many years have you practiced as an OB/GYN?

- How many births have you attended?

Catherine Emily

- Which hospitals do you have access to?

- If I choose you, where would I deliver?

- Would you be available for the delivery, or would I be handed over to another doctor? Why?

- How many babies do you deliver every month?

- How many patients do you see per day? How long is each appointment?

- What are your views on the various birthing preferences and how do you accommodate your patients' preferences?

- Have you had any experience with high-risk pregnancies?

- How many C-sections have you performed? How many C-sections do you perform in a month?

After asking each of these questions to your list of three possibilities, now ask yourself some questions as well:

- Did you like the doctor's communication style?

- How was their bedside manner?

- Did the rest of the staff seem helpful and friendly?

- How was the office? Was it clean?

Expecting First Time Moms

- Is the office conveniently located?

- Did you have to wait long to be seen?

With these questions answered, you can now settle on the doctor that you feel is right for you and get started on your prenatal visits.

Your prenatal appointments should ideally begin at eight weeks of pregnancy. Your first prenatal visit will typically be the longest. This is the familiarization meeting where your doctor gets to find out everything, they need to know about you. It is vital that you arrive ready to answer all the questions that the doctor might have. These will include questions on your medical history (including family medical history), birth control methods, last menstrual period, medications you're taking and/or allergic to, among others.

During your first visit, your obstetrician will also conduct an array of tests. These include a Pap smear test and several blood tests. These tests will be performed to ascertain your health status, for your benefit and that of your child. The blood tests, for instance, will be done to determine your HIV status, hemoglobin levels, blood type, Rhesus factor, sickle cell status, and even your Rubella status.

It is critical that you are entirely truthful with the doctor during the first visit (and the subsequent ones as well) as this will give them a full understanding of you and your medical history. Prenatal visits are neither the time nor the place for bashfulness. Be open with the obstetrician, answer questions, and volunteer any helpful information that you might have. The more information the doctor has on you, the better they can help you. If you are unsure about anything (for instance, your family's medical history), say so. Don't make things up for the sake of answering. You might be putting yourself and the baby at risk.

Based on the outcome of your laboratory tests and the consultation, you should expect to get some guidelines from your doctor regarding:

- Allergies, medications, dental care, diet, and environmental hazards

- Travel and physical (exercise, sex) limitations, if any

- Prenatal vitamins and supplements

- Miscarriage precautions

Before leaving your obstetrician's office, make sure to ask whom to call in case of an emergency. You should also get clarification on what constitutes an emergency. This will also be your chance to get a schedule in place so that you know when you are expected to be at your obstetrician's office throughout the next nine months.

Usually, a healthy pregnancy will require fewer visits during the early stages and progress to more frequent visits as you approach the delivery date. A typical schedule for a healthy pregnancy will involve one prenatal visit a month from week four to week 28, one prenatal visit every two weeks from week 28 to week 36, and finally, one prenatal visit per week from week 36 to week 40 and beyond.

Certain risk factors will necessitate deviating from the typical schedule. These include being thirty-five years and older and/or having preexisting health problems. Medical problems that arise during the pregnancy, for example, preeclampsia, will also require that you visit your obstetrician more often for closer monitoring.

After your first prenatal visit, your subsequent visits will be pretty much similar. They will involve your doctor monitoring your blood pressure, weight gain, the baby's growth, and heart rate. Your doctor will also keep an eye on your hands and feet to check for swelling. Later, as the pregnancy advances, your doctor will recommend ultrasounds at appropriate times to check for any birth defects and even to check the gender if you wish to find out. The ultrasound to check gender might be repeated later for confirmation, especially if the baby's positioning left some room for doubt.

Some of your prenatal visits will also require that you undergo special tests to check for gestational diabetes and other conditions. This is more so if you have a history of certain medical conditions in your family. It is also during the prenatal visits that you'll receive any vaccines that you'll require. An example of a vaccine that you'll be offered is the whooping cough vaccine, which you will get between weeks 27 and 36. These vaccines are administered to protect you and your unborn baby.

You can keep a notebook in which you'll record any questions you need to share with your doctor during your visits. Pregnancy brain (the forgetfulness that comes with pregnancy) is a thing you might struggle with. Your notebook will come in handy in ensuring you do not forget any important things that you might want to consult with your doctor on.

First-time moms will usually be excited to get started on their prenatal visits as soon as possible. However, before eight weeks, there's not much to be done during a prenatal visit. During the first one to eight weeks after conception, the most an obstetrician can offer is a confirmation of pregnancy and maybe a general health check. This should put you at ease because it means you have at least eight weeks to grab yourself Dr. Right if you do not have one already.

The exception to the rule is if you have had any health complications or consider yourself a high-risk pregnancy. In this case, you should get yourself to an obstetrician soonest possible after the home pregnancy test turns positive. This will ensure that you get the medical attention you require immediately to alleviate any risks to you and the unborn baby. If you have been taking any long-term medication, you'll also want to consult with a doctor immediately after finding out that you are pregnant. This is because some medicines can be harmful to the baby, and you'll need to know what your options are as far as managing your condition vis-à-vis ensuring baby's safety.

If you already have preferences in terms of how you intend to approach your birth, you need not be tied down by that when choosing an obstetrician. Most medical professionals are ready and willing to accommodate the views and preferences of expecting moms. You only need to have an open discussion where you let your doctor know how to envision your birth to be like. For instance, your perfect doctor does not need to be a hypnobirthing expert just because you are interested in hypnobirthing. You can make it work either way.

Choosing an obstetrician who is a good fit for you the first time helps you have an easier time with your subsequent births should you choose to have multiple children. Women who use the same obstetrician for their multiple children have an easier time during prenatal visits as they do not have to explain their medical history all over again. They also settle into an easy, solid, and comfortable relationship with their doctor, a fact that can be very reassuring to an expecting mom.

Chapter 3:
The Morning Sickness Remedy

Nausea and vomiting are two of the earliest signs of pregnancy. Unfortunately, for some women, these two unwelcome guests make themselves comfortable well into the pregnancy, sometimes continuing into the second and third trimester. Morning sickness is the term that is used to refer to nausea and queasiness that occurs when a woman is expecting a child. This nausea comes about because of the sudden increase of hormones in the body. This dramatic shift in the hormones is beneficial to the development of the unborn baby. It is a different ballgame for the expecting mother.

Morning sickness is named so because the symptoms are likely to manifest during the early hours of the day. For many women, this is the case. It is necessary to note that morning sickness can happen at any time of the day and night.

When it does happen, morning sickness can take away the joy from a pregnancy. It is uncomfortable and has been known to impact a woman's appetite negatively. It cannot be very comforting to know that anything you eat will be thrown up a few hours later. If you are experiencing morning sickness, you can take specific steps to feel a little better. You might be unable to rid yourself of nausea and vomiting completely, but you can take small steps to alleviate the severity of either or both.

The first thing you'll want to do is take a good look at your diet and find out if you're eating anything that might trigger morning sickness. Common culprits include caffeine, spicy foods, and fatty foods. If you have always enjoyed your cup of coffee, it might be time to switch to something milder like tea. Toss the fast food and opt for some blander alternatives that are high in proteins and carbs. Some women report being triggered by seafood so you might want to check how you're reacting to this as well. The trick is to avoid any foods that are overwhelming in terms of flavor and aroma, as these have a high potential to cause morning sickness.

In their absence, you'll want to ensure your diet remains balanced and somewhat enjoyable, for your sake and the baby's as well. Go for foods that are mild flavored but rich in nutrients. These include cooked vegetables such as carrots or squash and fruits. Carbohydrates such as rice and baked potatoes are also nourishing and do not trigger morning sickness. You'll also want to keep some ginger nearby if you are struggling with morning sickness. Ginger has been shown to alleviate morning sickness, and you can have it in your tea or even bake some ginger cookies to snack on during the day.

Catherine Emily

As mentioned earlier, when morning sickness moves in, your appetite might move out. While you might not feel like eating, it is critical that you do. Your body needs the nourishment, and most importantly, your baby needs it too. The trick is to ensure that you eat small meals spaced throughout the day. Instead of having three large meals, have several small meals and snacks throughout the day. Drinking enough fluids throughout the day also helps. As with the food, ensure this is taken in small quantities as getting too full on fluids or food will make you feel queasy. Your body will be more receptive to cold liquids so ensure you put some ice in your drinks and take small sips throughout the day.

Tiredness will make your morning sickness worse, so ensure you get plenty of rest at night and even during the day. Schedule naps during the day, take breaks when you need to, and get to bed on time. While your body is changing and the baby inside of you is growing, you will be using up lots of energy. Resting ensures that you replenish your energy supply. In the morning when you wake up, do so slowly. Getting up and out of bed suddenly can trigger nausea.

As far as triggering nausea, exhaustion goes hand in hand with stress. When pregnant, it is essential to avoid stress as this hurts you and the baby. If you're struggling with morning sickness, stress is an even greater enemy. Stress hormones will only make the symptoms of your morning sickness worse. There are various ways of combating stress. One is to avoid stressful situations and environments. The other is to calm your mind using tried and tested means such as meditation and relaxation exercises. Chamomile tea is also a great relaxer and will send you straight to sleep.

Besides your diet and lifestyle, other factors could contribute to your morning sickness. Strong perfumes and fragrances, for instance, can trigger queasiness. If you seem to feel particularly nauseous in the bathroom, consider replacing all the scented soaps and shampoos with unscented products. Forego your powerful deodorant and stay away from the body splashes for a while.

Most women will have morning sickness only for the first trimester, after which the symptoms go away. For other women, morning sickness lasts throughout the pregnancy. As an expecting mom, it is vital that you're aware of the differences between morning sickness and another more severe condition known as hyperemesis gravidarum.

Hyperemesis Gravidarum

Hyperemesis gravidarum, abbreviated as HG, is the more severe cousin of morning sickness. It is a pregnancy complication that occurs in some women and can have dire consequences if not treated. If you suspect that you have HG, you should head to a hospital immediately for medical attention. Failure to do so can lead to severe dehydration which is harmful to you and your baby.

If you experience any of the following signs and symptoms, you might be suffering from hyperemesis gravidarum:

- Nausea that is always accompanied by severe vomiting

- Nausea that does not subside or go away as the pregnancy progresses

- Severe dehydration

- Inability to keep any food down

- Extreme fatigue

- Jaundice

- Low blood pressure

- Increased heart rate

- Headaches and confusion

Depending on the type of hyperemesis gravidarum that you have, you could either get medication or be hospitalized. Mild cases will require you to take certain meds and observe dietary and lifestyle changes. For severe cases, a hospital stay will be necessary so that you can receive fluid and nutrition through an intravenous line (IV).

Some women will get relief from hyperemesis gravidarum as their pregnancy progress. For others, this complication will require management throughout the pregnancy. If you fall into this category, there are several treatment options available to you to make you as comfortable as possible. One of these is acupressure.

Acupressure focuses on the pressure point that reduces nausea, thus stimulating the body to heal itself by applying the right kind of pressure through massage. Some women will opt for acupuncture, which is often more effective than acupressure when it comes to activating the body's healing ability. Both acupressure and acupuncture are ideal treatment options as they are not detrimental to the mom or baby.

It is important to note that morning sickness differs from woman to woman and from pregnancy to pregnancy. As such, while you might have an easy first pregnancy with little to no morning sickness symptoms, this could change with your second baby. The solution is to be alert to your triggers, and then make the necessary changes that will ensure you get as comfortable as possible during your pregnancy journey. In case of uncertainty, always consult. As with the prenatal visits, keep a notebook if you must. Writing down when you felt most nauseous can help you identify patterns. You can after that use this information to come up with lasting solutions, including determining the foods that seem to trigger your nausea.

Quick Snacks for When You Have Morning Sickness
When you're dealing with morning sickness, sometimes all you'll want are practical recipes that you can quickly whip together. Morning

sickness will not be such a drag when you know you can kick it to the curb with a five-minute recipe. Consider preparing any of the following snacks when you cannot seem to keep anything down:

Ginger Cookies

Ginger cookies can be quickly baked at home using carefully measured portions of all-purpose flour and ground ginger. You can also add other spices such as cinnamon and cloves, but only if they do not make your nausea worse. If you are not up to the task of baking, you can stock up on store-bought ginger cookies, at least until you're able to bake.

Lemonade

Many pregnant women find that lemonade settles their queasy stomachs, so try making some at home. Home-made lemonade is much better than store-bought as you can control the amount of sugar that goes in. You can also substitute sugar with a healthier alternative like honey. Not only is lemonade great for making you feel less nauseous, but it's also packed with vitamin C, which is an antioxidant. Coupled with some ice cubes, a glass of lemonade will help you feel refreshed and settled in no time.

Coconut Water Smoothie

When going through morning sickness, you'll likely be getting dehydrated from losing so much water. Coconut water is precisely what the doctor recommends as far as keeping you hydrated. Not only is it naturally hydrating and so sweet to the taste, but it also contains five electrolytes that are needed by the body. These are sodium, magnesium, potassium, phosphorus, and calcium. The body needs these electrolytes for the healthy function of cells, nerves, and tissues.

To make coconut water even more interesting, make a smoothie with bananas and strawberries. Make sure the strawberries to clean the berries thoroughly as you do not want to introduce pathogens in your body. Bananas are rich in several vitamins and minerals including potassium and vitamin B6 while strawberries are an excellent source of vitamin C.

Vegetable Soup

You can make an easy vegetable soup using readily available vegetables such as cauliflower and zucchini. If you like, throw in some celery and carrots as well. To avoid making the soup too bland, throw in some seasoning like garlic, bay leaf, and even oregano. Vegetable soups are nourishing and gentle on your sensitive stomach, which is precisely the sort of balance you need in your life right now.

Banana-Oat Muffins

You can never go wrong with bananas and whole oats. These are easy to prepare, and you can make a batch of them to last you the entire week. For best results, use wholegrain rice flour. Wheat flour can easily irritate some people's stomachs, and you do not want to be taking chances when you're pregnant.

Easy Fix Fruit Salad

If you're only able to keep down fruit, make sure it is good fruit. While you cannot survive on fruits alone, sometimes, all you need is a refreshing bowl of fresh fruit salad. The best fruits to eat during pregnancy, especially when facing morning sickness, are those that are refreshing and packed with vitamins. Watermelon, for instance, is packed with vitamins A and C, iron, and calcium. Watermelon is 90% water, which means it is also highly hydrating. Other fruits that you should include in your salad include oranges, mangoes, avocados, bananas, and apricots. A fruit salad is a good snack to carry to work with you as it is easy to make in the mornings and doesn't spoil easily when stored well.

Chicken Salad

A chicken salad is easy to prepare and makes for a good snack or even a whole meal depending on the portion. To make chicken salad, you'll need a baked chicken that has been cut into small pieces. You'll also need mayonnaise, celery, lemon juice, and pepper. If you like, you can add grapes and almonds as well. Chicken salad is a wonderful recipe in that it is something that you and your partner can have for dinner without getting worried about monotony. You'll only need to make sure that you switch up the ingredients and you'll be good to go.

Quinoa Salad

Quinoa is a superfood that contains proteins, iron, all nine essential amino acids, and B vitamins. It makes for an excellent source of nutrients during pregnancy. To make a quinoa salad, cook quinoa first in a saucepan of boiling water. It takes about ten to fifteen minutes for quinoa to cook well. Once done, strain and rinse with cold water, making sure that all moisture has been removed. Transfer the dry quinoa to a salad bowl and toss in whatever you wish. This could be onion, tomato, olive oil, pepper, and parsley. The best thing about this salad is that you can have it as many times as you like without compromising on your nutritional requirements.

Greek Yogurt Snacks

Greek yogurt is rich in protein and highly nourishing. When pregnant, it is recommended that you give more priority to Greek yogurt, if you can, as you'll get more nutrients this way. To make Greek yogurt interesting, consider using it as the replacement for certain items in your everyday meals. For instance, use Greek yogurt as a salad dressing, or as a replacement for sour cream in quesadillas. Adding Greek yogurt to pancake mix makes your pancakes filling and wholesome, especially if you opt for wholegrain flour.

Chapter 4:
Exercising Do's and Don'ts

After finding out that you are pregnant, you'll probably start to wonder where certain things fit in your life. Take exercise for instance. If you were highly active before pregnancy, you'd likely be wondering whether you need to slow down or even just quit. As a rule of thumb, exercise is recommended during pregnancy. Exercise is beneficial to pregnant women in various ways. For starters, exercise releases endorphins which are the hormones responsible for making you feel happy and relaxed. It's common for pregnant women to suffer mood swings during pregnancy, and the feel-good hormones throw a delicate balance to the mix. Exercise during pregnancy helps to ease some of the physical discomfort experienced by expecting moms by stretching your muscles and preventing cramping. Staying active is also a great way to prepare the body for labor and delivery, which are two very physically demanding tasks. Think of exercise as the warm-up and labor and delivery as the main events.

However, exercise during this period calls for reason and discretion. If you were playing impact sports before, you might want to consult with your obstetrician before continuing with the same. There have

Expecting First Time Moms

been instances where expecting moms who are professional athletes have been given the go-ahead to compete in their respective sports while pregnant. The decision mainly depends on your doctor's assessment of your safety and that of your baby. If you led a majorly sedentary lifestyle, your first trimester might not be the time to start training for a half-marathon.

Thirty minutes of exercise in a day, on average, is enough time for ensuring your body remains in good shape. If you led a majorly sedentary lifestyle before you got pregnant, you could start exercising by walking. Walking is always an excellent way to exercise as it is cheap and readily available. You do not need any special gear for it, and you can easily fit it in your daily schedule. It is also easy on the body as it is a low-impact exercise. It is also easy to tag along interested parties and worthy companions into a thirty-minute walk than it is for other forms of exercise.

Speaking of low-impact exercise, another option you'll need to investigate is yoga. Prenatal yoga is a safe, healthy exercise option for expecting moms that can help to reduce stress and improve sleep. Prenatal yoga also boosts the strength and flexibility of your muscles, which ultimately helps with the labor and delivery process. Prenatal yoga can also help with back pains, headaches, and even morning sickness. A thirty-minute session of prenatal yoga might be precisely what the doctor recommended. Not only does your physical well-being get a boost, but you'll also get the chance to bond with other expecting moms.

If yoga is not for you, or if you feel yoga is not enough, you can still get your recommended daily dosage of exercise through other means. Swimming, for instance, is a great way to exercise your entire body during pregnancy. Swimming comes highly recommended for expecting moms and other demographics as well, mainly because it is one of the quickest ways to boost your cardio-respiratory fitness.

Indoor stationary cycling and low-impact aerobics are other options you can investigate. Whatever you decide on, it is vital that you keep the following do's in mind:

- Wear comfortable, loose-fitting clothing, including a supportive sports bra

- Go for shoes that are designed for the type of exercise you are engaged in

- Stick to flat, level surfaces to minimize chances of injury

- Make sure to eat enough calories to meet the energy requirements of the exercise and pregnancy as a whole

- Eat at least one hour before exercising

Expecting First Time Moms

- Keep a water bottle nearby for use before, during and after the workout

- If you need to get up during floor exercises, do so slowly to avoid feeling dizzy

As far as ensuring your well-being and that of your baby during exercise, observe the following don'ts:

- Don't engage in physical activities where falling is a possibility.

- Contact sports or activities where abdominal trauma can occur should be avoided.

- Do not participate in activities that require you to hold your breath for extended periods.

- Do not exercise in hot weather or humid temperatures.

- Do not exercise until you are exhausted; exercise during pregnancy should be done in moderation.

- Do not shock your body by engaging in intense activity after a long period of zero activity.

Before engaging in any physical activity that you fear might impact your baby, always consult with your obstetrician. It is crucial that you obtain your doctor's go ahead before getting started on any physical activity. During pregnancy, your body will change significantly. One of these changes is an increase in oxygen requirement to meet the needs of your developing baby. The increase in hormonal levels in your body will also cause your ligaments to stretch. When these ligaments that support your joints stretch, your risk of injury goes up. Lastly, you'll also experience a shift in your center of gravity because of the increase in weight and its uneven distribution. What this means is that you are more likely to lose your balance and fall over.

While you may have consulted and gotten the green light to exercise, you should still be on the lookout to determine how your body is responding. There are sure warning signs that indicate that it's time to stop exercising and speak to your doctor. These include:

- Shortness of breath
- A decrease in fetal movement
- Headaches
- Muscle weakness
- Abdominal pains
- Lightheadedness
- Vaginal bleeding
- Sudden swelling of your ankles or face and pain in your calves

Expecting First Time Moms

As your pregnancy progresses, you'll probably find yourself dialing down the exercises and settling for your earlier options such as walking. This is okay and encouraged. In fact, during the last few weeks of your pregnancy, you'll want to combine some low impact exercise with lots of rest. This helps to keep the blood flowing while conserving the energy that you'll need for labor and delivery.

After delivery, it is essential to wait until your body is ready before going back to exercise. It is usually recommended that moms who have had vaginal births to wait six weeks before having a go at physical activity. If you have had a caesarian section, you'll need to wait at least eight weeks. Even though you might feel ready to jump right back to exercise immediately after delivery, it is best to wait for the recommended period to lapse. This is because while you may feel okay, your body still needs time to recover. Carrying a human being to full term for nine months is no mean feat for your body. A lot of changes will have happened within you, and your body will need to readjust to this new status minus the tiny tenant.

Labor and delivery have an impact on your physical well-being, including triggering pains such as lower back pain. Your pregnancy hormones will also linger in your body for up tu six months after delivery. These hormones increase your risk of injury. As before, you'll need to discuss your plan to go back to rigorous exercise with your obstetrician.

Catherine Emily

Whenever you feel ready to get started on some physical activity, start small by engaging in activities such as swimming, cycling, walking, yoga, Pilates, and even low-impact aerobics. Do not push yourself or hold yourself to extraordinarily high standards. If you are not ready to get moving, do not do it. Take your time. Even pushing the baby's stroller is enough exercise for a new mom.

Chapter 5:
Sleeping the Right Way

As you progress in your pregnancy and your bump grows bigger, you will soon realize that you will be required to make several concessions in your life. Your favorite clothes will get replaced by the more practical maternity jeans and tops, and your high heels might take a break. In their place, you might find yourself preferring less flattering footwear. Another area where you'll need to make compromises is your sleeping style. Expecting mothers need a lot of rest. This means you'll probably be sleeping a lot, sometimes even when you feel like you should not be. Increased levels of progesterone in your blood are responsible for most of the sleepiness that you'll feel, especially in the first trimester. Later, in your pregnancy, especially in the third trimester, this hormone and the exhaustion of carrying a baby will combine to keep you feeling sleepy most of the time.

There are various reasons why sleep becomes crucial when you are pregnant. First, rest is your body's downtime; a period where your body undergoes repair and maintenance. Your body will need to get enough repairs done when it's dealing with the increased demands of growing a baby. Your body is a machine, and any good machine must sometimes be shut down for repairs so that it can keep functioning well. Sleep also ensures the body is better placed to react to insulin. Your body's responsiveness to insulin is vital in keeping gestational diabetes at bay. Unfortunately for you, you might not be able to sleep as you always have. Some things will have to change.

The increased size of your abdomen and back pain are just two of the reasons why you might find yourself more uncomfortable in bed than you'd wish. Heartburn, shortness of breath, and even insomnia are others. Keep in mind that your baby will also have their own sleep schedule that might not be in line with yours. As such, while you're desperately trying to fall asleep, your baby might be keeping you awake with their nocturnal activities. During your third trimester, your baby will be big enough to deliver painful kicks and jabs. At this point, falling asleep might be harder than you thought. These are just some of the reasons why pregnant women get less sleep than their non-pregnant counterparts.

Fortunately for you, there are tips and tricks you can use to ensure that your sleep (and sanity) remains intact during your pregnancy journey. For starters, have a sleep schedule. The human body is impressive in that it can quickly adapt its clock to align to your sleeping patterns. Train yourself to wake up at the same time every day and go to bed at the same time every night. Once your body clock is attuned to this schedule, you'll find it easy to fall asleep every night. As a matter of fact, you'll see your body guiding you to sleep on those nights when you've stayed up past your bedtime. Waking up early and refreshed will allow you to have a productive day, and at the end of the day, your body will be ready to rest. This cycle is highly essential in ensuring good physical and mental health.

The second thing you should do is get enough exercise during the day. Exercising during pregnancy alleviates the symptoms of pregnancy that might make you too uncomfortable to sleep at night. These include leg cramps. Exercising also ensures that your muscles are adequately stretched, and your blood is flowing well, both of which are vital for a relaxing sleep. Stick to low-impact exercises such as walking, yoga, and swimming, and you'll have no problem falling asleep at night. A bonus of exercising is that you might be so tired that you'll have no option other than to just fall asleep.

Having a soothing nightly ritual before bed is another way to ensure that you fall asleep faster when you finally get to your bed. This ritual could be anything from a warm bath to a relaxing cup of chamomile tea or even some meditation before sleeping. Alternatively, do all three! The idea is to wind down before bed and get yourself in the right mindset for a good night of some restful sleep. There are various online resources that you can use to access guided meditation material including videos and audios which you can save to your laptop or phone for reference when necessary. You could even download sleep apps to your phone. These come with tips on how to fall asleep better and relaxing music and sounds.

Limit the bed to the activities it was initially intended for, which is sleep and sex. If you are continually watching TV or using your smartphone in bed, the brain will associate the bed with those two activities. As a result, you'll always find yourself wide awake and alert when you should be sleeping. If you limit the bed to sex and sleep, the brain stores those two activities and associates the bed with them. As such, every time you get inside your bed, the mind will only be thinking of only two things. For a pregnant woman, one of those two activities will almost always carry the day.

If you are one of the women who experienced a heightened libido during pregnancy, use it to your advantage. Sexual intercourse is an excellent way to ease tension from your body and relax into a deep sleep. This relaxation can be attributed to the increased levels of oxytocin and the decreased levels of cortisol in the body. Oxytocin is a hormone that is sometimes referred to as the love hormone and is responsible for the social bonding that occurs when two people are affectionate with each other while cortisol is the stress hormone.

Making your bedroom as comfortable as possible is another way of ensuring that you sleep more easily when you are pregnant. When you are pregnant, a lot of things will make you feel uncomfortable. One of these is too much heat. Strong smells are another culprit. Whatever it is that makes you uncomfortable, ensure that it has been completely removed from your bedroom. Turn your bedroom into a sleep sanctuary. Take away everything that you don't like and replace them with the things that make you feel happy, safe, and comfortable. Turn down the heat by leaving the windows open or sleeping with a fan on. You're more likely to fall asleep when the room you are sleeping in feels like your haven.

Some women find that they are no longer able to sleep in their bedrooms, regardless of how comfortable and relaxing the bedrooms are. If this is the case, sleep where you feel most comfortable, even if it is the floor of the living area. Pregnancy is an interesting time in that you'll catch yourself having weird preferences, but the best thing to do is go along with them if they do not compromise your safety and that of the baby. If you no longer wish to sleep next to your snoring partner, change arrangements. Go with the flow and wait it out. After the pregnancy hormones stabilize, you'll find yourself returning to your normal self. At this point, you can return to your matrimonial bedroom and make amends with your beloved.

As far as sleeping positions, the best way to sleep during pregnancy is on your side. Bend your legs and knees, and then put a pillow between your legs. Better yet, sleep on your left side as this encourages the flow of blood and nutrients to the placenta and the baby. If you experience back pain while sleeping on your side, place an additional pillow under your abdomen. If you are struggling with heartburn, propping your upper body with pillows will help. You'll go through a whole lot of pillows while pregnant. A particularly handy pillow that you'll come across is the maternity pillow. Maternity or pregnancy pillows come in various sizes and shapes, but they all work similarly. They provide much-needed support and cushioning to you and your bump to ensure you are comfortable as you sleep.

You do not have to sleep in one position throughout the night; switching is fine. However, you must avoid sleeping on your back and on your stomach while pregnant. When you lie on your back while pregnant, the abdomen rests squarely on your intestines and your major blood vessels. This hinders proper circulation of oxygen and nutrients in your body and to your baby as well. The weight on your abdomen could also overwhelm your back, resulting in back pain. You might also find it hard to breathe properly while sleeping in this position. Sometimes though, you'll wake up in the middle of the night and discover that you accidentally rolled over and slept on your back just because it's what you were used to pre-pregnancy. When this happens, you should not panic. A few hours of accidentally sleeping on your back cannot harm the baby.

On the other hand, sleeping on your stomach is just plain impractical, especially when you are further along in your pregnancy. While some women can sleep face down during the early days of pregnancy, this position is soon abandoned as the bump grows more prominent. If you are very keen on sleeping with your face down, there is a pregnancy pillow that can help you do so. This pillow has been designed with consideration being given to your growing bump. It comes with a donut-like hole in the middle where your bump can rest as you snooze face down.

If you aren't getting enough sleep during the night, for whatever reason, it is crucial to schedule naps during the day. This way, you can get all the rest that your body needs. If you are unable to sleep entirely at night, do not spend hours tossing and turning in bed, as this will only lead to frustration. Instead, get out of bed, and do something relaxing that you enjoy like reading a book or having a cup of peppermint tea. Do not self-medicate with sleeping pills or any other medication while you are pregnant. This could harm your baby. You could ask your doctor to prescribe sleeping aids that are safe for you and baby.

Ensure that you take your meals at appropriate times so that they do not interfere with your sleeping schedule. Being too full just before bed can make sleep uncomfortable. Lying down on a full stomach is the perfect recipe for heartburn. On the other hand, eating several hours before bedtime might mean contending with hunger pangs when you go to bed. It is ideal to eat at least two hours before bed. If you feel hungry after that, you can take a light snack like milk and whole oatmeal cookies to sustain you throughout the night. Certain foods will keep you alert and jittery and interfere with your ability to fall asleep well. These include foods with too much sugar or caffeine content.

While getting enough sleep is critical, do not set a stopwatch and demand from yourself eight or ten hours of sleep just to accomplish this goal. Watching the clock is the surest way to go crazy. Sometimes, it's best to listen to your body and just respond appropriately. If you feel energized after only six hours of sleep, then sleep for only six hours. If you are picking up the signs given by your body, you'll be fine.

Later, after the baby comes, you might find yourself not sleeping as much as you wish. Night-time feedings and a crying baby are not exactly conducive to sleeping. During the day, try as much as possible to take naps when the baby sleeps. This might be hard for the first few weeks when you feel like you have a million things to do when the baby is sleeping. However, you should be aware that you need this sleep as much as you needed it before the baby was born. Lack of sleep can make your mothering experience a dreadful one. Sleep during the day and sleep at night if you can. Alternate night-time care with your partner so that you can have reasonable amounts of sleep.

Chapter 6:
Nutrition and Top Foods to Eat

What you eat during your pregnancy will have a profound impact on you and your baby as well. As a pregnant woman, you have increased demand for calories, and you'll find yourself wanting to eat more and more. Your growing baby needs the right nutrition in terms of vitamins, minerals, and proteins to develop well. Your body also requires the right food so that it can be up to the task of growing a human being. At the same time, you want to ensure that the food you are eating allows you to lose the weight you'll have added when the baby is finally delivered. As an expecting mom, one of the best things you'll do for yourself is ensuring you eat foods that are wholesome and as natural or organic as possible. There are various categories of food that you must ensure are included in your diet so that you can meet all your dietary requirements.

Dairy Products

During pregnancy, you'll have an increased demand for calcium and protein which can be met by consuming the right dairy products. If you haven't already, stock up your fridge with dairy products, especially yogurt. Greek yogurt is an excellent bet as it contains higher calcium levels than most dairy products. Consider adding non-fat milk too to your diet and some types of cheeses such as cheddar and mozzarella. Soft cheeses are not recommended for pregnant women as they can contain listeria bacteria which can use infection. Listeria bacteria causes listeriosis which may be fatal to your unborn baby. If you are lactose-intolerant, you can still get your calcium from other alternatives including soymilk. Some people who are lactose intolerant can sometimes tolerate yogurts, especially the probiotic kind.

Eggs

Eggs are sort of the MVP of health foods, as they come with a little bit of everything. A large whole egg contains 77 calories, protein, fat, vitamins, and minerals. Eggs also provide an essential nutrient known as choline. Choline is vital for boosting metabolism and ensuring a healthy nervous system. Pregnant women who are allergic to eggs can get the choline that their bodies and babies require by replacing eggs with alternatives such as liver and turkey heart. Quinoa and amaranth also have significant amounts of choline. If you decide to go for liver, ensure that you take only small amounts of the same. This is because the liver contains very high levels of vitamin A, and too much of it can harm your baby.

Avoid eating raw eggs when pregnant as these could be contaminated with Salmonella. Foods that commonly contain raw eggs include home-made mayonnaise, lightly scrambled eggs, cake icings, and salad dressings.

Dark, Leafy Vegetables

Dark leafy vegetables contain vitamin A, vitamin K, and vitamin C. Vitamin A is an essential vitamin that ensures the proper development of the immune system and the eyes and skin. Vitamin K is critical for ensuring blood clotting in the event of injury, thus preventing excessive bleeding. On the other hand, vitamin C is an essential vitamin that has significant benefits to the human body. For a start, vitamin C is a strong oxidant that strengthens your body's immune system. Vitamin C keeps at bay high blood pressure and heart diseases and can help improve iron absorption in your body. This vitamin is also crucial in ensuring your memory remains sharp, which is a plus, especially when dealing with pregnancy brain.

Besides the vitamins, dark leafy vegetables also contain iron which is required for blood production. Iron is a key component in the production of hemoglobin which is the component of your blood that carries oxygen throughout your body. Consuming enough portions of dark leafy greens while pregnant is also a great way to get enough fiber in your body. Fiber helps with constipation, which is a problem that many women experience during pregnancy and even after delivery.

Lean Meat

Meat is a source of high-quality protein, during pregnancy and beyond. When pregnant, it is important that you stick to lean meat that has been cooked well. While you may have enjoyed a fat, juicy rare steak before pregnancy, your preferences will need to change during pregnancy. Eating fatty foods including fatty meats can harm your baby's immune system. At the same time, eating meat that is undercooked can present a considerable risk to the baby by making them susceptible to the toxoplasma parasite. The Toxoplasma parasite is a parasite that causes an infection called toxoplasmosis, which can affect the brain, lungs, eyes, heart, and liver. This infection can spread to your baby with dire consequences if not caught and treated in good time.

Whole Grains

A whole grain is any grain that comes complete in terms of containing the endosperm, germ, and bran as it came from the fields. Whole grains differ from the refined grains in that refined grains have only the endosperm. The reason why refined grains get a bad rap is that during refinement, all the critical nutritious stuff is removed and what you are left with is just starch with small amounts of protein. The important and healthy components of grains are contained in the germ and bran. This means that when you opt for whole grains, you get to eat the most useful parts which are nourishing to your body. On the other hand, binging on refined grains only helps you pile up the carbs.

Whole grains contain several vitamins including thiamin, folate, and niacin and minerals such as iron and magnesium. They also contain dietary fiber and proteins. Consuming a diet rich in whole grains can help prevent colon cancer and diabetes and reduce the risk of heart disease and Alzheimer's disease. Eating whole grains during pregnancy is a great way to set a wholesome foundation for your baby.

Some whole grains that you can look out for during your next grocery shopping trip including whole wheat, whole oats, rye, brown rice, buckwheat, quinoa, and corn.

Avocados

Avocados are one of the loveliest fruits of this planet. Not only are they so versatile in the ways they can be incorporated in a diet, but they are also packed with useful vitamins, minerals, and healthy fats. The healthy fats of avocados are useful for the development of your baby's skin, brain, and tissues. The potassium levels of avocados are also excellent in combating pregnancy cramps. You can never eat too many avocados when you're pregnant, so make sure you make that salad, have that avocado toast, go for that guacamole…the options are endless!

Legumes

There are many different types of legumes, but some of the healthiest and most common options include chickpeas, lentils, kidney beans, black beans, soybeans, peanuts, and navy beans. Legumes are a readily available and cheap source of fiber and B vitamins. B vitamins are all the vitamins found under the vitamin B complex group. They include thiamin, riboflavin, niacin, pantothenic acid, pyridoxine, biotin, folic acid, and cobalamin, which are usually indicated as vitamin B with a number suffix. These B vitamins are essential in ensuring the body's nerve and blood cells are healthy and are crucial in the formation of genetic material and DNA.

Fruits

Dried and fresh fruits should be incorporated in your pregnancy diet as often as is possible. Dried fruits such as almonds, dried apricots, cashew nuts, dates, dried figs, and raisins are an excellent source of fiber, vitamin A, iron, magnesium, vitamin E, and vitamin C, among others. The natural sugar of dried fruits is an excellent source of energy for your body while you'll need during this time. You must be careful though-dry fruits contain many calories which could lead to weight gain. Over-indulgence in dry fruits could also lead to constipation and flatulence.

Fresh fruits, on the other hand, are excellent sources of vitamin A, C, and fiber. Consider including mangoes, oranges, pears, bananas, and berries in your pregnancy diet. Fresh berries are packed with antioxidants. They are also fleshy and juicy and can help you stay hydrated.

Salmon

Pregnant women are generally advised to avoid fish that have high mercury content. Mercury is a metal that can have detrimental effects on the human body, and especially on an unborn baby. Such effects include damage of the nervous, digestive, and immune system and the kidneys as well. In instances where the levels of mercury are incredibly high, the consequences might be fatal. Fish which have been shown to contain high levels of mercury include tilefish, swordfish, king mackerel, and shark. Fortunately, salmon happens to be on the list of fish which is safe for consumption during pregnancy.

Salmon contains omega-3 fatty acids, proteins, vitamins, and docosahexaenoic acid (DHA). Omega-3 fatty acids are crucial for improved cardiovascular health while DHA is vital for the development of the baby's brain. The proteins and vitamins in salmon are beneficial when it comes to muscle growth and repair and increasing immunity.

During pregnancy, salmon should be eaten when well-cooked. You can broil, poach, or bake it. It is best to avoid raw salmon as in the case of sushi as this could place you at risk of bacterial infection. It is also necessary to ensure that you get your salmon from a trusted source.

Water

It's not really a food, but it highly ranked during your pregnancy. It is crucial that you stay hydrated throughout your pregnancy. Staying hydrated is one of the most important things you'll do during your pregnancy, and you must also ensure that your water source is trustworthy too. Water ensures that the essential nutrients are delivered to your baby, prevents UTIs and constipation, and can also help with fatigue and headaches. If you were not really a big fan of water before you were pregnant, you might want to get yourself a water bottle that you'll carry around and sip from all day.

During the first trimester, some women will find it hard to keep down even plain water. If you fall into this demographic, you might find it hard to stay hydrated. In such cases, it is necessary to investigate other alternatives including Hydrolytes Ice Blocks or poles. If the plain taste of water puts you off during pregnancy, try flavoring your water with fruit. Slices of citrus fruits like oranges and even berries are ideal. Ensure that the fruits have been washed thoroughly.

Sweet Potatoes

These two starches are ideal alternatives to wheat, as they contain good carbs and sugars that are safe for your body. Sweet potatoes are high in beta-carotene. Beta-carotene is what is converted by the body to vitamin A. vitamin A is required by the body for the proper functioning of the eyes, immune system, and reproductive systems. Sweet potatoes can be made into sweet potato flour, allowing you to bake your favorite pastries without worrying about gluten.

It can seem overwhelming at first, all these things that you are required to eat during pregnancy. It can especially be difficult in the first trimester when you must deal with nausea and morning sickness and cannot seem to keep anything down. However, you can make it easier for yourself by trying some tried and tested tips that have worked for other moms.

For a start, create a pregnancy meal plan. A meal plan is a simple way of ensuring that you always know what to eat and when. You will not have to go through the hassle of coming up with a creative new meal every day. Instead of having large meals that have been crafted to meet all your dietary requirements at once, spread your portions throughout the day. Snacking on healthy bites at intervals is a much better approach than stuffing yourself in one sitting. Small portions will also keep away nausea and heartburn.

While it has been consistently said that pregnancy is a time when you must eat for two, this is not entirely accurate. There is no pressure to overeat for the sake of overeating. Eat healthily and listen to your body. When you are full, take a break, and do something else. Your body has ways of communicating when you need to eat more, namely hunger pangs. You do not need to clear two full bowls of oatmeal for your baby to grow well. Eat well and in moderation, and especially so when you start to get those constant cravings. Giving in to all your cravings can be detrimental in the long run.

Lastly, always consult with your doctor if you are in doubt about something. There exist a lot of pregnancy-related myths online and even in social circles, and it's always best to bust them with the help of a professional.

Chapter 7:
Tips to Curb Cravings

It is common to experience food cravings during pregnancy. Thanks to all the hormones wreaking havoc in your body, you're likely to find yourself desiring the oddest foods at the oddest of hours. You're not alone. A lot of expectant mothers have found themselves in similar shoes. Typically, cravings appear at the same time as morning sickness and then wane off as the pregnancy progresses. Cravings are usually the strongest during the second trimester. Some expecting moms develop a craving for one thing that lasts throughout the pregnancy, while others will crave one thing today and a different one the next day.

For starters, it is essential to know that even science does not exactly know what causes food cravings in expectant moms! Up until this point, science has only been able to make some educated guesses. One of these guesses purports that food cravings are your body's way of ensuring you get the vitamins and minerals that you and the baby need during the pregnancy period. Another school of thought says that since you're overloaded on hormones, you might interpret smells and tastes differently. That nasty pickle that you could not stand pre-pregnancy suddenly taste like heaven. Nobody said pregnancy was going to be simple!

As a pregnant woman, it is critical to ensure that you pay attention to what your body is telling you. Craving a specific type of food might mean that your body is lacking a nutrient, which you can often get in a different kind of (healthier) food. For instance, if you find yourself craving chocolate, it's likely because you lack magnesium. You can get magnesium in bananas, dark leafy veggies, and even in nuts and grains. That is not to mean that you should never indulge your chocolate cravings occasionally. The idea here is to ensure you strike a balance between the healthy and the not-so-healthy.

There are tips that you can use to ensure that you are not overwhelmed by your cravings.

Eating more frequently is a great way to ensure that you do not confuse hunger with cravings. As an expecting mom, you'll often be hungry, sometimes even immediately after eating. During this period, your body is quickly processing whatever you take in and sending it where it's needed most. It is vital to ensure that you supply your body with what it needs when it needs it. Eat the required three meals per day, with a focus on breakfast. Breakfast is the most important meal of the day, and a good breakfast sets a good pace for the rest of the day. In between, snack healthily to ensure you are getting the nutrients that you need. Do not put in very long gaps between meals, and do not overindulge in junk food. Remember to give your body the hydration it requires by drinking lots of water after and in between your meals.

Ensuring you take a protein at every meal and snack is another tried and tested way of kicking cravings to the curb. Not only are proteins vital as they are the building blocks of life, but they also keep you feeling sated, thus ensuring you do not crave anything else. Consider adding healthy protein options such as Greek yogurt, eggs, and even nuts to your meals, paired with some healthy carbs that are low in sugar and high in fiber. This will keep away the cravings for a reasonable amount of time, after which you can snack on something else or occasionally give in to the craving.

Getting enough exercise and rest is an excellent way of managing your food cravings during pregnancy. When you are tired, your body tends to be sluggish and may function abnormally. You might end up desiring foods that are no good for you just because you are exhausted and out of it. It is critical that you exercise well and sleep well during pregnancy so that your body is in top condition. The rush and relaxation you get from exercise could very easily replace the sugar rush that you think you want.

Distract yourself from your food cravings by indulging in activities that take your mind away from food. If you're sitting idly in the house all day, you are likely to make frequent trips to the fridge. If you leave the house to walk the dog, go for yoga classes or even catch up with other expecting moms, you are likely going to forget about your cheesecake craving, even if only for an hour or two. Do not give up control over your life to your cravings.

Keep in mind that overindulging your cravings could result in a lot of weight gain, something that you might struggle with post-delivery. Sugar and junk food are two culprits that you need to be especially aware of. While you should not obsess over every pound gained during pregnancy, it is essential to be mindful of what your cravings are doing to your body. With this bigger picture in mind, you can put in place a plan to ensure you do not pack on unhealthy pounds just because you could not say no to your cravings.

Sometimes, when it comes to defeating your cravings, you'll need a partner to help you out. Put in place a plan on how to deal with your cravings, and have your partner reinforce this. Your partner could assist in various ways including portion control or even replacing the unhealthy snacks with some healthier options. Your partner could also just be that voice of reason reminding you that you can only eat so many ice-cream tubs before they become harmful to your body.

Some women will experience cravings for non-food items during pregnancy. For instance, some women will experience a strong desire to snack on items such as clay or even dirt. These types of cravings are referred to as "pica". If you strongly feel like snacking on laundry starch, do not do it. Talk to your doctor. It is likely that your body needs a nutrient, and your doctor can help you identify this and lead you towards a healthier alternative.

It is important to understand which cravings healthy and which ones are aren't. If you are craving fruits and certain veggies during pregnancy, you can happily give in to these. There is really no harm in indulging in lots of fresh fruit during pregnancy, if the fruit is properly washed. In the case of dry fruit, eating too much might cause constipation. Sometimes, cravings aren't bad at all. They can do you and your baby lots of good. On the other hand, craving soft cheeses and sushi will not have the same effect as craving fruits. This is because some foods like soft cheeses and sushi are not recommended for pregnant women as they can cause infection.

A parallel phenomenon to food cravings is food aversions. During pregnancy, you might suddenly find yourself repulsed by certain foods for no good reason at all. You might suddenly hate the smell or look of a food, even to the point of nausea. Food aversions, like food cravings, get better with time. Unless your aversion is keeping you from getting a particularly essential nutrient, it should not bother you.

Some of the foods that women commonly develop aversions to during pregnancy include garlic, eggs, onions, and even tea and coffee. If you are averse to foods that are required for the healthy development of the baby, ensure you get these nutrients in other ways. For example, if you cannot stand meat in the first trimester, make up for the deficit by eating high-protein nuts. You might also want to ensure you eat the food you hate by hiding it in something else. For example, if you cannot stand eating your vegetables, throw them in your smoothie next time you make one. This way, you'll get the nutrients you require without getting sick.

The beauty of the human body is that while some things are common for most people, everybody is different in the way it functions. As such, you might find yourself not having any cravings or food aversions during pregnancy. It is normal for a pregnant woman not to have cravings. If you are feeding well, you should not be worried about the absence of cravings. Make sure to eat healthy wholesome foods and take your vitamins and you'll be just fine.

Chapter 8:
The First Trimester, Weeks 1 to 12

The first trimester of your body announces itself in a big way. First, you'll miss your period. This is usually the first cue that you might be gaining the title of a mother in the coming nine months. Second, you are likely to deal with morning sickness, which could range from mild to terrible in terms of severity. You are also likely to be undergoing other unpleasant conditions such as flatulence. Because the first trimester is counted from week 1 to week 12, you might very well be into your first trimester by the time you find out that you are pregnant! This is because most women will usually take a pregnancy test four weeks after their last period, especially if the period is regular. If your period is irregular, you might be halfway done with the first trimester before you find out.

Lots of changes happen during this first trimester, and this is not just for the mother but the baby as well. The first trimester is when the baby goes from a fertilized egg to an embryo to a fetus. After conception, your unborn baby will be just a fertilized egg hoping to be properly implanted onto the wall of your uterus. But first things first, how do conception occur? Most people are generally aware of how conception takes place, thanks to high school biology and sex education. The magic of how your baby came to be, however, is in the details. So, what happens after ejaculation?

During ejaculation, a healthy adult male release anything between 40 million and 1.2 billion sperms. (This means that the child you are carrying is literally one in one billion). Because the vagina is an acidic environment that is not favorable to the survival of the sperm, the sperm is encased in a protective gel by the semen. Later, this gel is liquefied by enzymes that are produced by the prostate gland. This liquefaction occurs so that the sperms can be freed to travel to the eggs that are waiting to be fertilized. The freed sperms travel upwards and onwards until they get to the cervical mucus that stands guard at the entrance of the uterus.

During ovulation, the cervical mucus, which is usually acidic to keep stray sperms at bay, changes to become friendlier and more welcoming to the sperm. The mucus also acts as a reservoir where the sperms can hang out for a few days before being declared useless. This is usually for five days.

After the sperms have made it inside the uterus, they are pushed towards the fallopian tube by uterine contractions. The first sperm enters the fallopian tube minutes after ejaculation. Unfortunately, that first one is rarely the fertilizing sperm. You can think of this sperm as the recce sperm or the curtain raiser for the swimmer that will eventually carry the day.

In the meantime, the eggs that were produced during ovulation have been undergoing their journey as well. These eggs are transported from the ovary through the fallopian tube, where they await the lucky sperm. Transportation of the eggs is more graceful, with the finger-like fallopian tubes sweeping them along until they get to a junction of the tube known as ampulla isthmus. This graceful journey takes a little bit longer than that of the sperm-thirty hours to be approximate. Once the egg gets to this junction, it rests for another thirty hours. Fertilization must occur during within these thirty hours. Otherwise, the egg will no longer be viable. For the sperms that make it to the fallopian tube, it is a game of chances as far as knowing which one will fertilize the egg. The egg rests in the tube for as long as thirty hours in order to allow for full fertilization and to allow the uterus to prepare to receive the fertilized egg. After the thirty hours, the fertilized egg begins its descent to the uterus.

An egg contains a membrane that has receptors for human sperm. This membrane also plays a protective role in ensuring a fertilized egg cannot be fertilized by another sperm. This is because the membrane, scientifically known as zona pellucida, becomes impermeable post-fertilization.

You must be wondering, what about twins and triplets? Well, in the case of twins, this occurs when the fertilized egg splits into two or when two eggs are fertilized by two different sperms. In the former, the result is identical twins, while the latter case produces fraternal twins. Now, back to the baby-making class...

A fertilized egg undergoes a series of transformations before it can be called a baby. The first few days after fertilization is a period of multiple cell division, otherwise known as mitosis. The outcome of the mitosis is a mass of very organized cells that are known as a blastocyst. The blastocyst is what is implanted in the uterus, and this usually happens after it has hatched out of its protective membrane (the zona pellucida). While all this is happening, you might be completely unaware of the new life developing inside of you. However, sooner rather than later, your menses become a mystery, and you realize that indeed, you are going to be a mother.

By the time the blastocyst is implanting onto your uterine wall, you are probably four weeks along into your pregnancy. After this, you can expect your hormone levels to increase. This is because the blastocyst has hormonally signaled the ovaries to stop producing more eggs and instead produce estrogen and progesterone. These hormones ensure that you do not receive your period and boost the growth of the placenta. At week five, your baby is basically three layers, which will later form the important organs of the baby including the skin, the circulatory system, and the internal organs including lungs and intestines.

Week six marks a critical development period for your baby as it is when the spinal cord, brain, and heart develop. The eyes, ears, and upper limbs begin to make their debut, albeit slowly, and your baby starts to take on that so very familiar C-shape that you've probably seen in many fetal illustrations.

At week seven, your baby's face starts to peek from beneath the multiplying cells. The nostrils start to take shape, and so do the retinas of the eyes. Lower limbs start to form, and the upper limbs grow more pronounced.

Eight weeks into your pregnancy, your baby will have a nose. Tiny fingers will have started to form on their upper limbs, while their lower limbs will follow closely, developing into distinguishable paddles. Between weeks nine and ten, the parts of the body that have formed will become more defined. Your baby will also grow, even though its head will appear bigger than the rest of its body. At week 11, your baby's external genitalia begin to form into either a penis or clitoris. At the end of week 12, your baby has a more developed face, fingernails have started to form, and the baby weighs about 14 grams. By the end of the 12-week period, the risk of miscarriage is considered to have reduced significantly.

Expecting First Time Moms

It is important to take great care of yourself during this first trimester as it sets a pace for the rest of your pregnancy. By the twelfth week of your pregnancy, you should have seen your doctor at least once. Your doctor will give you professional guidance on how to care for yourself during your prenatal period. They will assess your health and even that of your baby to ascertain the state of your pregnancy. If yours is a high-risk pregnancy, your doctor will discuss your options on how to best care for yourself and the fetus during this critical period.

The first trimester is a period where you might have to deal with a whole lot of morning sickness. Usually, for most women, morning sickness gets better after the first trimester. Chapter Three of this book delves deep into morning sickness and gives you tips that you can use to combat the same.

Because this is such a significant event of your life, you might find yourself feeling overwhelmed during the first trimester. Between the hormonal shifts and dealing with the shock and excitement of being a mother, it's normal to feel conflicted. It is important that you maintain a good support system for yourself during this period. Be open with your partner, family, friends, doctor and anyone else that is willing to listen. Acknowledge your feelings and emotions, talk about them and work through them. It might seem very confusing at the start, but things tend to get better as you move along the trimesters.

Chapter 9:
The Second Trimester, Weeks 13 to 26

Most expecting moms are happy to get into the second trimester of their pregnancy, as it tends to be the most comfortable of the three. During this second trimester, you'll most likely have overcome the uncomfortable signs of pregnancy including morning sickness. Your appetite will most likely be back, and your energy levels will be looking good. Some expecting moms will also experience an increased sex drive during this trimester. Most of your clothes will still fit in the second trimester. This is the one trimester where you can make the most of your pregnancy before the exhaustion and discomfort of the last trimester kicks in.

Your baby will also be making the most of this trimester as well. In the second trimester, your baby makes great strides in terms of their development. At the end of your first trimester, your baby will be about four inches long and weighing in at an ounce. You can expect this to go to twelve inches and two pounds at the end of the second trimester. Quite some impressive growth! What this means for you is that you'll also be steadily gaining weight as you consume enough food to make up for baby's demands. The steady weight gain of the second trimester should not concern you if you are eating healthily. Once the baby is out, you can quickly shed off the extra pounds through exercise.

So, what exactly happens to your baby during this second trimester period? Your baby's limbs which started developing in the first trimester are usually well defined by the time you hit the second trimester. Their genitalia are also fully developed, and you can now schedule an ultrasound to check your baby's gender. Your baby is also starting to become their own person-they can yawn, make faces, and later, they'll start making good use of their little legs and arms by throwing some most adorable jabs and kicks.

Your baby's hair will start to grow at week 16, and by week 22, they'll have a decent amount of hair, including eyelashes and eyebrows. Because the baby's digestive system was fully formed by the end of the first trimester, the second trimester is all about putting it to practice. Your baby will now start practicing for life outside of your womb by sucking and swallowing. They can even taste the food you eat at this point, so make sure you snack on the healthy stuff if you are hoping to influence his preferences.

The second trimester marks a period of refinement and re-organization for your unborn, with most of the organs developed during the first trimester being fine-tuned. For instance, the ears and eyes will be moved to their correct positions during the second trimester. The brain will start to control their heartbeat-which has previously beaten spontaneously-and their eyelids as well, allowing them to blink. In short, your baby will be starting to function like a little normal human being.

What to Do During the Second Trimester

As an expecting mom, there are several things you can do during the second trimester to ensure that you are entirely in control of your pregnancy as is humanly possible. One of the things you need to investigate is amniocentesis. At week 15 of the second trimester, consider scheduling multiple marker tests to check for any chromosomal abnormalities. The window of opportunity for the testing of these abnormalities is typically between weeks 15 and 20. It is vital that you get your unborn baby screened so that you are prepared for what to expect. In the case of severe abnormalities, your doctor will discuss your options with you.

Another thing you'll want to decide is whether you want to find out the gender of your baby. Some parents are excited to find out, while others like to keep it as a surprise until delivery time. Whatever the case, the second trimester affords you the luxury of choice as far as the gender reveal is concerned. By this time, your family and friends already know you're expecting as you'll likely to have announced after the first trimester. Even the ones you haven't told yet will be able to make out a noticeable baby bump. The choice to check your baby's gender should be yours to make and not brought on by the pressure of an impending baby shower or gender reveal party.

While you haven't started feeling physical discomfort during the early second trimester days, you can bet it is coming. Invest in comfortable sleepwear during your second trimester. This could be anything from some comfy pajamas to a body pillow. If your mattress or bed isn't comfortable enough, consider changing to a better alternative. You'll be glad you did this while your bump was still reasonably sized. Later, as your baby grows and you progress to the second trimester, mobility might be a challenge. So, get comfortable now. Store the nuts for the winter while you can still move them, so to speak.

Second-trimester preparations will also include signing up for a childbirth education class, either alone or preferably with a partner. Such courses fill up quickly so the faster you can get into one, the better. Besides childbirth classes, don't forget to also engage in activities that you enjoy. Yoga, Pilates, walking, reading books, napping, and staying hydrated are essential. Do not neglect the little events that you enjoy. With your child-free days quickly coming to an end, it is imperative that you relish this alone time while you can.

The second trimester is an ideal time to get started on decorating the baby's nursery. If you already know whether you are getting a boy or girl, you can paint the nursery in hues and tones that will appeal to them. Even if you've chosen to keep the gender a surprise, you can still tastefully decorate the nursery in neutral colors. Alternatively, go for the road less traveled and go for whatever colors you prefer, traditional gender stereotypes aside. Whatever it is that you choose, make good use of the energy levels of the second trimester. A time will come in the final trimester when all you want to do is nap all day, and you will not do the nursery any justice then.

Besides getting the baby screened, you'll also want to be tested as well. If you have a medical history of it or are at risk, get checked for gestational diabetes. Your doctor will do this by scheduling a glucose screen, which usually happens between weeks 24 and 28.

Other things to consider during the second trimester include narrowing down on the baby name options, going for one last trip or babymoon, and arranging for post-maternity leave childcare if you are planning to resume work.

At the end of week 26 of the second trimester, you'll likely find yourself feeling more discomfort that you did at the beginning of the trimester. Hormonal fluctuations, swelling, and headaches might become the norm. Prioritize your well-being in terms of exercise, staying hydrated, and eating healthily, and consult with your doctor in case you are worried about something. You might also start to experience another pregnancy phenomenon-the Braxton Hicks contraction.

Expecting First Time Moms

Braxton Hicks contractions are the body's way of preparing for labor. You'll know you are experiencing them when your abdomen or groin areas tighten and then relax. These contractions can be mild or strong, and even though they begin as early as seven weeks, you'll not likely feel them until later-maybe 16 weeks or so. Braxton Hicks contractions are sometimes referred to as "false labor". If your Braxton Hicks is making you uncomfortable, try lying down or going for a walk, depending on what you were doing before they started. Taking a relaxing bath or a massage can also help.

As your pregnancy progresses, false labor can be very concerning, especially to a first-time mom. Call your doctor if you are worried about the contractions you are experiencing. You should especially call your doctor immediately if the contractions are followed by vaginal bleeding, leaking of fluid, and noticeable change in baby's movements and/or severe discomfort that you cannot "walk off". If you experience continuous contractions that come five minutes apart in an hour, call your doctor or midwife immediately.

Chapter 10:
The Third Trimester, Weeks 27 to 40

The third trimester of your pregnancy journey starts at the end of week 27 or the beginning of week 28 and lasts until you give birth. This could be up until week 40 or even later. Some women have been known to have a delay of up to 42 weeks or more. This is to be expected and should not be cause for worry unless your doctor says otherwise. Some babies require just a little more time, while others are ready to make their debut on their exact due date.

During this last trimester, you will probably be moving slower or even less, and you'll be wondering if you could possibly get any bigger. The answer is yes! Your baby is not done growing, and in the coming weeks, you'll feel and look bigger. As the third trimester ends, your baby will be approximately 50cm long and at 7.5 pounds will weigh as much as a small pumpkin.

Your baby transforms quite a bit during this last trimester. For starters, their cartilage changes to bones. This is your cue to ensure that you keep consuming as much calcium as you can to ensure the proper development of your baby's bones. Foods that contain calcium include dairy products such as milk and yogurt, and dark, leafy greens as well. Oranges are also a source of calcium. Instead of opting for store-bought orange juice, go for organic oranges in all their farm glory. If you find it hard to eat oranges, make your own orange juice at home using a blender or juicer.

The other thing that will be changing in your baby is the skin. Throughout the first and second trimester, your baby will have a translucent skin through which you can see their organs. In the third trimester, your baby's skin becomes opaque. They will also start to accumulate fat under their skin as they prepare for their debut in the big world. As a result of these changes, the vernix, and lanugo that have previously protected your baby will start to shed, their way of taking a back seat as new protectors come into place.

It will likely please you to know that your baby's five senses are fully developed around week 30 of pregnancy. Now is your chance to sing to the baby, introduce the baby to your loved ones, and even play with a flashlight shone over your belly. Your baby will now have a sense of what is happening in the outside world, and you'll probably notice them react when your partner starts talking to you. As your baby grows and becomes more alert, you'll notice the kicks and punches becoming more powerful and, in some instances, painful. This is set to continue until the last weeks of pregnancy when the movements become more subdued as the baby grows bigger and starts running out of space.

The third trimester is also a period of significant development for your baby's brain. During this trimester, your baby's brain starts to test some skills including blinking, regulation of body temperature, and dreaming. It can be surprising too many to learn that unborn babies dream. After all, what experiences do they have to dream of? It is a fact however that unborn babies and newborns dream of what they are familiar with and that is the sensations that exist in the womb.

Your baby's first poop starts to build up in the baby's intestines in the final weeks of pregnancy. This poop is referred to as meconium and is a mix of blood cells, lanugo, and vernix. Your baby will take this first poo a day or two after they are born. In some instances, the baby will poo in the womb. When this happens, an emergency C-section is usually recommended to ensure that the baby's airways are not blocked by the meconium. Meconium staining is just one of the several causes of fetal distress. Other causes of fetal distress (when baby's oxygen supply is compromised) include placental abruption, umbilical cord compression, and maternal illness. Placental abruption is said to have occurred when the placenta separates from the uterine wall during pregnancy. This separation is dangerous as it means the baby is unable to receive the oxygen delivered by the placenta via the umbilical cord.

As the third trimester nears to an end, your baby will drop lower in your pelvis in readiness for being born. This phenomenon is known as

Expecting First Time Moms

lightening and can occur two to four weeks before delivery in first-time moms. Dropping does not necessarily mean that you're about to go into labor anytime soon. At your antenatal appointment, your doctor will check how far the baby has dropped. In some instances, the baby might drop with its feet or bottom instead of its head. When this happens, the baby is said to be in breech position.

A baby in breech can be handled in several ways. One of them is to deliver the baby as it is with the buttocks or feet coming out first. Breech births are not a favorite of most doctors and moms as they can compromise the well-being of the baby. This is because easing the baby's head from the birth canal becomes harder when it's the last thing that delivered. As the baby's legs and bottom are delivered, the cord can easily wrap around the baby's neck thus cutting off oxygen. This risk posed to the baby is the main reason that most doctors will recommend either turning the baby and getting it settled in the headfirst position or going for a C-section.

While your baby readies herself for the outside world, your body will also be undergoing a variety of changes. For starters, on a very general level, you'll be feeling very uncomfortable. You'll find it hard to move as fast as you used to, you might feel big and bloated, and you'll be making even more frequent trips to the bathroom than you used to. As your bump grows to accommodate your growing baby, you might start to experience cramps or sharp pain around the abdominal area as the ligaments stretch. There is not much you can do about these pains besides lying down and taking it easy when they happen.

Besides feeling uncomfortable, you'll also feel exhausted during your last trimester. Pregnancy is a highly demanding task on a human body, and nine months of it is no joke. To deal with fatigue, eat well, get some exercise, and get enough rest. While you might feel like it's a ridiculous suggestion to exercise when you feel so tired, it is for the benefit of your body that you keep moving. Exercise releases endorphins which can make you feel more positive and energized. Staying active also helps your body get ready for the very physical activity that is delivery.

Heartburn is another problem that is commonly experienced by pregnant women during the third trimester. As your bump gets bigger and bigger, your uterus tends to push your stomach and its contents upwards leading to heartburn. Heartburn can be highly uncomfortable and painful. The milder cases of heartburn can be treated at home using tested methods such as eating small meals several times per day instead of one large one and using over the counter antacids. Severe cases of heartburn should be attended to by a doctor, who may recommend other options such as prescription H2 blockers. H2 blockers are medicines that are used to treat conditions related to excess stomach acid. Sitting upright and standing are known ways of maximizing space in your abdomen. Whenever you can, avoid lying down too much and especially after eating.

Expecting First Time Moms

False labor, otherwise known as Braxton-Hicks contractions, can be very concerning during the third trimester. Your baby is big enough to survive in the outside world and any sign of labor, true or false, can send a first-time mom running to the delivery room. During the third trimester, Braxton-Hicks contractions will make a somewhat regular appearance in your day to day life. As you near delivery, it is important to have familiarized yourself with the signs of true labor. True labor occurs in contractions that have regular intervals, that usually become stronger as time progresses. True labor cannot be quietened with movement, which is typically the case for Braxton-Hicks. True labor comes with back pain and usually some vaginal discharge. You may also notice the passage of the mucus plug that blocks the cervical opening. If you are experiencing true labor, get in touch with your doctor. If you are experiencing false labor (which is the opposite of true labor), go for a walk or lie down.

While in your third trimester, you should start putting the final touches to your delivery plans. One of the things you'll need to do is investigate your maternity benefits and apply for maternity leave if you have not already. Maternity leave can be taken anytime from at least four weeks before delivery, although this might be subject to your specific region's employment and labor laws and your employer's policies.

The third trimester is also an appropriate time to decide what kind of birth you prefer if you have not already. Some women prefer to give birth in a hospital while others would much rather go for home births. Some prefer vaginal birth and yet others are all for C-sections. While these conversations are best had earlier when you have enough time to consider all options, you can still decide in the third trimester. However, the longer it takes you to choose, the fewer your options will be. For instance, a home birth requires that you have a trusted midwife and doula to help you deliver your child. It is essential that you identify a midwife and doula earlier on in the pregnancy so that you can cultivate a respectful and comfortable relationship over the nine months.

If you are resuming work after delivery, finalize on your childcare options. Childcare options could range from hiring a nanny, finding a suitable daycare, or even enlisting the help of a family member. Make sure that you tie all the loose ends of childcare before the newborn comes along. It can be overwhelming planning things while taking care of a newborn who hasn't let you sleep in two weeks!

A lot of women experience a nesting urge during these last weeks of pregnancy. Nesting is the urge to clean things and organize them properly. As the due date nears, you might find yourself getting worked up over the state of the house or the nursery. There is really no scientific reason why the nesting urge affects some pregnant women. There are only good guesses as to why this might be the case. Anticipating the arrival of this brand-new family member can excite a soon-to-be mom enough to want to clean everything and everywhere. Sometimes, nesting can also be brought on by the fact that logically you know you will not have enough time to clean after the baby comes. You might feel an overwhelming urge to clean everything before the baby arrives because you know that logically you have more time to do so before the delivery.

If you are delivering at the hospital, the last weeks of the third trimester are an excellent time to pack a hospital bag for yourself and the baby. A hospital bag contains all the essentials that you will require for delivery and those that the baby will need after birth. These essential items include the hospital paperwork including your ID and insurance cards, bathrobe, socks, your essential oils, baby's clothes, a collection of your favorite relaxation music, your birth plan, and even your favorite pillow. When packing for the hospital, ensure you take into consideration what you'll require during the delivery and after. Some moms tend to pack for the labor and delivery, and the baby, and forget that they'll need some things for when the baby has already arrived. A more comprehensive list of what to include in your hospital bag can be found in Chapter 15 of this book.

Chapter 11:
The Stages of Labor

For a first-time mom, labor can be both an exciting and frightening experience. You've probably heard less-than-pleasant labor stories from friends, family, and even strangers online and are worried about your own experience. A good thing to remember is that every labor experience is different; no two births are identical. Even for you, if you decide to have multiple children, every subsequent delivery will vary from the previous. There are four stages of labor that every woman will undergo during childbirth.

First Stage of Labor: Early and Active Labor
The first stage of labor is commonly the most prolonged of the four stages and can last anything from a couple of hours to several days. This time tends to be shorter for subsequent deliveries. The first stage of labor is usually divided into two phases, namely early and active labor. Early labor is the onset of true labor pains, which involve the dilation of the cervix in preparation for the baby's debut into the birth canal. Besides dilating, your cervix will also soften and become thinner, a process referred to as effacement. While this is taking

place, you'll feel mild irregular contractions. You might even notice a clear or pink vaginal discharge. This discharge is caused by the disintegration of the mucus plug that forms at the cervical opening during pregnancy.

Most women go through early labor comfortably, with little to no pain. Your normal activities need not stop while in early labor, as you wait for the contractions to grow in frequency and intensity. For first time moms, it is natural to panic when true labor kicks in. There's no cause for alarm though, and you should only head to the hospital when the contractions become intense, if you're bleeding vaginally, or if your water breaks. The best way to stay calm during this stage is to get in touch with your doctor for updates and keep your labor support partner close.

You can also go for a walk, take a bath, or listen to relaxing music to keep calm and relaxed during early labor. Because of how unpredictable early labor is in terms of duration, you might be indulging in your bath, walk, or book for a long or very short while before you get into active labor.

Active labor is the phase of the first stage of labor where your cervix dilates wide enough to accommodate passage of a baby. Active labor is where the real work begins. When you are expecting, your cervix is usually about 3cm in length. When active labor sets in, your cervix will dilate to 10cm, up from the 6cm it dilated during early labor. Active labor involves more discomfort and stronger contractions. Most women experience leg cramps, nausea, and even pressure on their back. Active labor should ideally find you in hospital. If you haven't already gotten to the delivery facility by the time active labor kicks in, do so immediately. You'll need the medical experts by your side when going through active labor.

Typically, active labor lasts about eight hours, with your cervix dilating 1cm everyone hour. Some women are lucky to have shorter active labor periods. Try and remember everything you learned during the childbirth classes to ease your discomfort during active labor. If you require pain medication, ask for it. You are best suited to decide your pain threshold, and your doctor will be on hand to discuss your relief options with you. Taking a walk, getting a massage, and breathing between contractions will help you feel better during this phase. You could also have a warm bath and roll on a birthing ball.

The last fifteen to sixty minutes of active labor are referred to as the transition. During this phase, your contractions are very intense and close together. This is perhaps the most painful stage of labor, and you'll need all the support you can get. Expect to feel some pressure on your back and rectum areas, and at times an overwhelming urge to push. If you are not dilated enough, your obstetrician will advise you against pushing. This is because you might get too tired and cause your cervix to swell before the baby is ready to be delivered.

Second Stage of Labor: Delivery of the Baby

The second stage of labor follows closely behind the transition stage and is the stage when you deliver your baby. This stage calls for you to channel all the calories you indulged in during your cravings and push with all you might. For some lucky moms, the second stage of labor lasts only a few minutes. For others, this stage can last several hours. First-time moms tend to take longer to go through the second stage.

During this second stage, your doctor will instruct you on when to push and when to take a break. It is recommended that you take a breather between contractions. As a first-time mom, it is essential to determine what works best for you so you can push efficiently and effectively. Some moms will prefer to push while squatting; others will do it while on their hands and knees. Choose a position that works well for you and change this whenever possible, so you do not cramp up in one spot.

If you are wondering how pushing happens, think of it as having the most massive bowel movement of your life. This might sound gross, but it is the most accurate analogy. While the pain of the contractions might be overwhelming at this point, try your best to relax your body, and focus on the push. Release the tension from your face and shoulders and concentrate on getting that baby through the birth canal. Some moms will experience an overwhelming urge to push, and this is normal. Push as much as you need to, but don't be frantic about it.

When you feel a contraction building up, take a deep breath so that you can be prepared to push through it. If your obstetrician instructs you to stop pushing, pay attention and do as told. Sometimes, the doctor will ask you to take a break so that you can regain your energy. They could also do so to prevent the baby's head from being pushed out too quickly.

While you push and hope for the baby to be born quickly, the delivery team will be ensuring that they're ready for the baby's debut. They'll do this by arranging sterile drapes and instruments and donning their surgical scrubs and gloves. The delivery team will also monitor the baby's heartbeat throughout the labor period using a fetal monitor and give you the support that you need to deliver successfully. The fetal heartbeat is monitored so that the baby can be checked for distress as things can also get difficult for the baby during delivery.

After you've been in active labor and pushing for a while, a phenomenon known as birth crowning will occur. Birth crowning is the gradual emergence of your baby's head through your vaginal opening. Crowning signals impending birth and the period between crowning and delivery can be as short as ten minutes or less. If you need some motivation, you can touch your baby's head when it crowns or use a mirror to take a good look. Sometimes, all a pushing mom needs is some physical evidence of the gift awaiting them at the end of those contractions.

Expecting First Time Moms

After birth crowning, your baby's head will finally emerge from your birth canal, followed by the rest of the body. If your baby is stuck in your birth canal, your doctor can manually deliver the baby using forceps or other means. Once the baby's head and shoulders are delivered, your doctor or midwife will most likely suction their nose and mouth to get rid of amniotic fluid. Further suctioning may be done after the entire baby is delivered if your doctor deems this necessary. Suctioning helps to ensure that the baby does not inhale the fluid into their lungs.

After your baby is outside of your womb, it is essential to keep him or her warm as they are not able to immediately regulate their temperature. The doctor or midwife will place your baby on your abdomen to keep him warm and to help you bond. It is normal to be too tired to properly bond with your baby at this point. If this is the case, your birth partner can step in to ensure the baby gets some skin-to-skin warmth and bonding.

The baby's umbilical cord will also be clamped in two places, and a cut will be made between the two points. If your partner is present, they can do the honor of cutting the umbilical cord. The baby does not feel any pain while the cord is being cut since the cord does not contain any nerves. The reason why it does not contain any nerves is that it is not actually made of skin or connective tissue. Instead, the umbilical cord is formed from what is known as Wharton's jelly. Some doctors recommend waiting a few minutes before cutting the umbilical cord. This is to ensure that enough blood flows from the placenta to the baby, thus lowering the risk of newborn anemia. After the umbilical cord is cut, blood will be collected from it to determine the baby's blood type. This blood may be used for other tests as well.

One to five minutes after your baby is born, the medical team will carry out an assessment known as the Apgar assessment and give your baby an Apgar score. The Apgar score indicates your baby's readiness to meet the world without medical assistance. The evaluation will measure the baby's muscle tone, heart rate, breathing, and response to reflexes. If your baby scores well on the Apgar assessment, you will be able to keep him with you. If not, the medical team might take him away for further checks. When all this has been done, you'll be ready to proceed to the next stage of labor and delivery, which involves the delivery of the placenta.

Third Stage of Labor: Delivery of the Placenta

After the baby is born, you're likely to focus all your attention on the miracle lying softly in your arms and forget all else. But not so fast, you need to deliver the placenta as well. The placenta is a very useful reservoir for nutrients and oxygen that has been helping to nourish your baby in the womb. Now that your baby is out, this reservoir needs to come out too. After the delivery of your baby, your contractions will not cease immediately. You will continue to experience close but less painful contractions, and these will help you deliver the placenta. Placenta delivery typically takes five to ten minutes. Some women might take longer.

Your doctor will check to see if the placenta is intact after it is delivered. If it is not intact, the placenta remnants in your womb must be entirely removed to ensure you do not get an infection.

Fourth Stage of Labor: Recovery

The final stage of labor and delivery is the recovery. This starts right after you're done delivering the placenta and continues months after you go home. After nurturing an entire human being in your body, and pushing it out to the world, your body is not quite what it used to be. It is vital to ensure that it returns to its natural state for your continued well-being.

One of the things your midwife or doctor will do to kick-start the recovery process is to massage your uterus. Massaging your uterus is a technique used to prevent uterine atony which causes post-partum hemorrhage, a leading cause of maternal deaths worldwide. Uterine atony is a condition whereby the muscles of the uterus fail to contract after birth. A uterine massage contracts your uterus back to its standard size and contracts the blood vessels that were previously feeding the placenta. Besides the uterine massage, your doctor might also stitch you up if you experienced tears or had an episiotomy during delivery.

Your doctor will also check your vitals, which include your heart rate and blood pressure and if everything looks good, you'll probably only need some rest before you can start receiving visitors. Some moms will also experience intense hunger after delivery. With all the calories you'll burn during labor, you can indulge in your favorite meal soon after birth. Many moms claim that the first meal you have post-delivery will taste like the most delicious meal of all time even if it is just a simple peanut butter and jelly sandwich!

Two to three days of observation in a hospital are all you require if you've had a vaginal birth with no complications. If you have had a C-section, you might need to stay in the hospital longer so that the doctors can monitor your recovery from surgery. C-Section moms usually go home after three to five days, depending on each situation. After the two or however many days you need in the hospital, your doctor will give you the okay to head back home with the newest family member.

You'll need to take it easy once you get home. Eat lots of healthy foods, drink plenty of fluids, and get enough rest. The first few weeks post-delivery can be intense, and it's okay to feel overwhelmed physically and even mentally. Always reach out and ask for help whenever you need it and accept it when it is freely offered. For the first few days, focus on ensuring you and the baby are well-taken care of. Other tasks like doing the laundry and dusting all the corners of the house can be outsourced to a willing family member or housekeeper.

Chapter 12: Hypnobirthing

Ask any woman, even those who are not moms, and they'll tell you that labor and delivery are a harrowing experience. This is because pain is what women have been conditioned to expect. In films and television shows, labor is depicted as this horrific event, with the mom-to-be screaming her lungs out and a dedicated medical team instructing her to push as hard as she can. In female conversations about childbirth, there is almost an unwritten rule that the most horrendous labor story gets the prize. Granted, labor is not exactly a walk in the park. It also doesn't have to be a screaming fest of intense and excruciating pain. A woman can deliver her baby in an experience that makes them feel calm and in control. Hypnobirthing is the practice that seeks to give expecting mothers control over their childbirth experience, ensuring more relaxed and less painful labor.

If you walk into a delivery room armed with horror stories of childbirth, you'll be tense and fearful. This fear is counterproductive because it causes you to have an increased level of adrenaline in your body. Adrenaline interferes with the release of oxytocin, a hormone that is needed to progress labor along. When the production of oxytocin is affected, your labor will be longer. Hypnobirthing equips you with techniques for ensuring that you stay calm and allow the necessary hormones to flow naturally, thus ensuring your labor is not prolonged more than is necessary. Hypnobirthing teaches women that they can give over their bodies to the magic of birthing while maintaining control over their minds.

So, what exactly is hypnobirthing and how did it come about? Hypnobirthing is a term that is derived from the word hypnosis and birthing. Even though it includes the word hypnosis, you should not expect anyone to hypnotize you in the traditional sense of the word. There will be no swinging watches in the labor room seeking to send you to the other realm. The hypnosis that occurs during hypnobirthing is majorly self-hypnosis and would perhaps be more aptly named as meditative labor. You will be hypnotizing your mind so that it can positively endure the process of giving birth. Hypnobirthing focuses on three main techniques which are controlled breathing, meditation, and visualization.

The origins of hypnobirthing can be traced back to a British obstetrician named Dr. Grantly Dick-Read who came up with what is called the FTP theory. FTP theory stands for Feat, Tension, and Pain. In his approach, Dr. Dick-Read stated that fear causes tension which, in turn, causes pain. This pioneering doctor further argued that fear during childbirth causes blood to be diverted away from the uterus, which starves the womb of the oxygen it needs to deliver the baby.

When this happens, the uterus does not function as intended, and labor becomes a prolonged and painful experience. Dr. Dick-Read ended his theory on the note that 95% of labor pains are caused by fear and tension, and women would benefit from less painful labor by incorporating relaxation techniques in their childbirth process. While Dr. Dick-Read pioneered this theory, it was not until later that the term hypnobirthing came to be. Michelle Leclaire O'Neill coined this term in 1987 in the USA. O'Neill is a published author of many books on childbirth and is an expert on hypnobirthing and pregnancy.

Most childbirth classes teach expecting moms how to breathe during labor, but very few go into the meditation and visualization practiced in hypnobirthing. The next sections of this chapter explore in depth the concepts of controlled breathing, meditation, and visualization that every mom expecting to have an almost painless birth should be aware of.

Controlled Breathing

When a first-time mom who is afraid of childbirth goes into labor, the last thing they are thinking of is how to breathe calmly. Yet, this is precisely what they need to ensure that their labor and delivery is as enjoyable as is humanly possible. During fear and panic, breathing is a labored process. You're likely to be taking puffs and gasps which will do nothing for your body and the baby that is about to be born. Learning how to control your breathing, especially during labor, will give you back control over the pain you expect to feel when giving birth.

Controlled breathing is used as a relaxation technique in that it sends signals to the brain. These signals, in turn, let your brain know that you are not under any stress and no stress hormones should be released. Stress hormones can interfere with the release of hormones that are needed to progress labor. Controlled breathing usually focuses on the speed and depth of breath. Deciding whether to breathe through the mouth or nose is another way of practicing-controlled breathing.

During labor, it is advised that you breathe in deeply through your nose and exhale through your mouth. While exhaling, focus on releasing all the tension that has built up within your body. Tension and stress make it harder for the baby to come out because it tightens the muscles. At the early stages of labor, breathing is usually slow. Later, it might become lightly accelerated and progress to even faster paces when you are about to deliver. The idea is to have you as the expecting mom in control of how you are breathing, regardless of whether that's slow or fast so that you can 'breath the baby down' instead of pushing endlessly amidst screams and pain.

Meditation

In a world that is fraught with ups and downs, unpredictability, disaster, and worries, choosing to focus on the positive is an art.

Meditation is a technique that involves focusing your mind in a way that achieves calmness and relaxation. Meditation requires you to tune out the distractions happening around you and focus on achieving maximum mental peacefulness. For pregnant moms, this is a skill that is very handy. Luckily for you, you can learn meditation and practice until you get better, in time for your delivery.

The first step to meditation in hypnobirthing is to get into a comfortable position. If you are uncomfortable and dealing with aches and pains, your mind will be distracted, and you'll not be able to meditate properly. Put on some relaxation music and start the process of settling your thoughts. Start by focusing on the positive outcomes of the delivery and replace any feelings of fear with thoughts of positivity. Think of how beautiful and loved your baby will be. Take deep slow breaths and remind yourself that you'll soon be a mother to be a most incredible baby.

Practice meditation throughout your pregnancy so that you know what works best for you by the time you go into labor. Enlist the help of your partner so that you have a sidekick in your meditation journey. Your partner can also help you in other ways such as putting together a CD of your favorite relaxation music. When you positively prepare your mind for the task ahead, you'll find it easier to go through labor.

Visualization

Catherine Emily

Delivery rooms are not the fanciest of places and walking into one can be somewhat scary. Thankfully, you can imagine yourself in a different place if the delivery room is not doing it for you. Remove your mind from the present and think of how wonderful it will feel to have your baby in your arms. If you have a favorite place that you like to go, think of yourself as being there. If you need a trusted pillow or lip balm to help you visualize better, carry it with you to the hospital. Thinking of things that make you feel happier will help you labor more peacefully, which is something that every woman can appreciate.

A combination of controlled breathing, meditation, and visualization can make a huge difference when it comes to delivering your first child. Getting mentally ready for your baby is as important as preparing physically.

A hypnobirthing course is typically covered in five classes, which are two-hours long on average. You may begin attending classes at any time between weeks 25 and 30. Some women attend classes right until the very last week. This can be impractical for some, especially when you take into consideration time and cost commitments and the physical exhaustion of the third trimester. You can supplement classes with books and online tutorials, especially if you are constrained for time or money, or both. When it comes to hypnobirthing, you'll need a birth partner to attend it with you. Some childbirth classes feature only the moms. Hypnobirthing is different as the birth partners have significant roles in ensuring the techniques learned are put to good use.

In hypnobirthing, the birth partner lightly massages the mom in labor while reminding the mom of what they need to be doing. Many classes usually provide a handbook with all the phrases and techniques that the birth partner needs to remember during birth. You are also likely to get a hypnobirthing CD that you can play on repeat during birth.

Taking control over the birth process using hypnobirthing helps to reduce the trauma associated with childbirth. It is unfortunate that a lot of mothers are scarred for life by the experiences they undergo in the labor room. Fortunately, with hypnobirthing, you can ensure that you do not suffer nightmares after delivering your baby. Hypnobirthing does not promise to deliver zero pain, but it does promise to lessen the pain and make your childbirth memorable in a good way. Some quick tips to remember about hypnobirthing are:

- Hypnobirthing is recommended for first-time moms and moms who have delivered before

- Hypnobirthing can be learned as a home study course or by attending classes

- You can still receive medical intervention should you need it

- Hypnobirthing can be incorporated in any birthing plan

- Even if your doctor or midwife does not understand hypnobirthing, you can discuss your choices with them and get their support

- You can go through hypnobirthing on your own if you do not have a partner

Myths About Hypnobirthing That Are Not True

Unfortunately, as it is with most things, there exist several myths about hypnobirthing that confuse first-time moms and moms looking to give hypnobirthing a go. One of the most common myths is that hypnobirthing will cause you to be so out of it that you'll not even be aware of what is happening in the delivery room. This is incorrect. The idea of hypnobirthing is to get the mom in such a relaxed state that external stimuli do not bother her. It does not mean relinquishing control over to someone else. It means acknowledging that you're in charge and controlling the outcome of your labor.

Another common myth is that hypnobirthing makes labor so pleasurable that you'll want to get another child immediately. Hypnobirthing is not about eliminating pain; it's about preparing the body and mind to endure whatever pain comes your way. It is impossible to have a labor that is completely painless. Even if you take medication, pain is a very subjective and relative matter.

Lastly, there are certain pockets of people who believe that hypnobirthing is a woo-woo type of theory that is practiced by people who also encourage free-range parenting and other new-age theories. This could not be further from the truth. Hypnobirthing is premised on scientific facts regarding how the body reacts to various stimuli such as fear, and there are real benefits to be gained from opting for hypnobirthing.

Chapter 13:
Post-Partum Recovery

As an expecting first-time mom, you've probably gone through multiple books, blogs, videos, and even classes on what to expect during pregnancy and childbirth. It is natural to want to be unprepared. Unfortunately, a whole lot of the resources available to pregnant women focus on just that: pregnancy and childbirth. As such, lots of moms find themselves surprised when it comes to dealing with life after childbirth, and specifically, post-partum recovery. This chapter will focus on the surprises to expect after delivery and tips that you can use to recuperate faster and better after bringing your baby into the world.

After delivery, your doctor will advise you on how long you'll likely take to recuperate. Typically, if you have had a vaginal birth, it is estimated that you'll require six weeks to heal. For caesarian section moms, this period is usually 12 weeks. While this period estimate is given in good faith and based on historical data and years of medical research, you must keep in mind that bodies heal differently.

Expecting First Time Moms

During pregnancy, many women gain weight thanks to all the eating and snacking they do to keep up with their increased demand for calories. Right after delivery, a lot of women find themselves worried about this extra weight and what to do with it. The first week after delivery will see you shed some pounds when the retained fluids exit your body. However, for the pounds brought on by the fact that you gained during pregnancy, you'll need a different strategy. For many women, this strategy involves exercise. If you were reasonably active before you got pregnant and during your pregnancy, you can easily resume exercise a few days after childbirth especially if this was a vaginal delivery. However, you will need to ensure that this exercise is light and friendly to your body which has undergone a significant event. Always check with your doctor before getting started on any exercise.

Keeping an eye on your diet is another way of ensuring you lose the extra pounds and stop more from piling. A healthy diet will also ensure your body gets the nutrition it requires to heal and produce milk for your new baby should you choose to breastfeed. As a bonus, breastfeeding your baby is another great way of losing weight. This is because breastfeeding makes use of the fat cells stored in your body during pregnancy.

Besides weight gain, your libido is another issue you might have to deal with after delivering your baby. It is a common occurrence for new moms to lose their sex drive to the extent where they have zero desire to be intimate with their partners. There are several reasons for this. For starters, being a mom to a newborn is not exactly a walk in the park. You're likely to feel exhausted and even overwhelmed, especially when your new bundle of joy decides to cry all night. While in this state of fatigue, you are not likely to be thinking of bedroom antics with your partner.

Your new body image is another factor that can contribute significantly to a decreased sex drive. When pregnant, your body will change to include things that were not previously present. You might develop stretch marks, your tummy will no longer be as taut as it was before, and you'll likely add weight in places you'd rather not. Some women take a while to accept this new body, and this affects their self-confidence. A woman with a negative perception of their body is unlikely to want to strip naked and be intimate with their partner. If you are going through the struggle of accepting your new body, it is important to share your fears with your partner.

A good and supportive partner will reassure you and help you come up with ways to feel better about your body. For instance, you could sign up for exercise classes together. You could also try other ways of being physically close such as taking baths together. What's most important to remember though is that this is your new body because you are in a new phase of your life. You're a different woman, one with the esteemed title of mom. You cannot quite go back to your young, single, and child-free body because that is no longer you. The journey to self-acceptance after childbirth might take a while, but it is highly recommended that you get started on it.

If you are breastfeeding, you might experience a decreased sex drive due to a decrease in levels of estrogen in your body. When this happens, you might experience vaginal dryness which will make sexual relations unpleasant. If this is the case, consider using lubricant during intercourse. If your libido doesn't get any better after several months, you might want to see a doctor.

Post-Partum Depression

Post-partum depression, also known as post-natal depression, is a form of mood disorder that comes about after childbirth. PPD can affect both genders but is usually most common in new moms. This depression manifests itself in various ways including extreme sadness, low energy levels, crying episodes, irritability, and even changes in sleep and eating patterns. The unfortunate thing about PPD is that it can easily go unnoticed, leaving new moms suffering in silence. Unfortunately, this silence has ended fatally for some moms.

Scientists have pointed fingers at several things as the reasons why post-partum depression occurs in new mothers. One of these is the sudden and significant decline in hormones post-delivery. During pregnancy, the female reproductive hormones increase tenfold. After childbirth, these hormones -estrogen and progesterone- drop back to their pre-conception levels. These hormonal fluctuations can negatively affect a new mother, who, at the same time, is dealing with the exhaustion of taking care of a newborn. At the same time, new mothers also must undergo the psychological re-alignment of taking care of this new person who is totally dependent on them for their survival. When this happens, especially in the absence of a support system, a new mother can easily sink into post-partum depression.

Some groups of women are at a higher risk of suffering from post-partum depression than others. If you have a history of depression, you are more likely to suffer PPD. Younger mothers and mothers who were ambivalent about their pregnancies are also high-risk candidates for post-partum depression. Your home situation is another risk factor that could put you at a higher risk of developing post-partum depression. For instance, if you are living alone with limited social support or if you are undergoing marital conflict, you are likely to find yourself battling with depression after delivering your baby.

Post-partum depression is usually hard to self-diagnose because some of its symptoms mimic the usual baby blues that a woman undergoes after delivery. Baby blues are the mood swings that women go through during the period after delivery. These are majorly caused by the hormonal changes and the adjustment to motherhood. Baby blues are a somewhat mild form of post-partum depression and typically go away after two weeks.

If your baby blues persist beyond these two weeks and last well over a few minutes every day, you might be suffering from post-partum depression. If this is the case, you'll need to see a doctor who can recommend medication and counseling. Consider seeing a doctor if you persistently experience the following symptoms and signs after delivery:

- Excessive fatigue that doesn't seem to go away
- Difficulty sleeping even after trying all recommended remedies
- Feelings of worthlessness
- Suicidal thoughts
- Homicidal thoughts or thoughts of hurting someone else
- Feelings of hopelessness
- General lack of interest in life
- Loss of appetite
- Loss of libido that doesn't improve after a few months

Post-Partum Psychosis

Post-partum psychosis (PP) is a form of severe mental illness that some women suffer after delivery. This form of psychosis can happen out of the blue to women who do not have a history of mental illness.

Women who have PP experience hallucinations and can easily harm themselves and other people. For this reason, post-partum psychosis is almost always treated with medication and hospitalization. The good news is that PP can be treated, and the mother can easily resume their mothering role in their child's life.

Post-partum depression can easily go undetected as the mother can easily fake a smile when expecting guests or when hosting family and friends. However, post-partum psychosis easily announces itself. There will be delusions, paranoia, confusion, and a general shift in the person's normal behavior. As a new mom, you might not be aware that you have PP as you will have lost touch with reality. It is crucial that you accept the help offered to you by family and medical professionals during your post-natal period as most of it is well-meant. If you do not feel much like yourself after childbirth, be open to discussions on how you can get better.

Generally, whether you are afflicted by the blues or not after delivery, there are several things that you can do to ensure you recover well after childbirth. For the first few weeks after your delivery, find a way of relieving yourself of all your duties other than feeding your baby and taking care of yourself. The few days and weeks after delivery are not the best time to be hauling large loads of laundry or spring cleaning the house. Ask for help from your friends, family, and even partner. Hire a housekeeper if you can afford to. A time will come

Expecting First Time Moms

when you'll be able to do the heavy lifting and that time is not right after you deliver.

It is critical for new mothers to learn how to stand up for themselves. This means not having to apologize for your preferences and parenting style. If you wish to breastfeed or bottle feed your baby, do so without apologies. If you need to take a nap while friends and family are visiting the new baby, proceed with your nap unapologetically. As miraculous as parenting is, it also opens a whole new realm of critics who are ready to dissect all your moves. Responding to each critic is the surest way to feel drained.

Find a support group of new and experienced moms to draw strength from. You might be comforted to know that little Jess isn't sleeping through the night either. There's always something you can learn from other mothers that will make your motherhood journey easier. This is especially true down the line when you need some of those tried and tested home remedies for dealing with colicky babies and teething problems. Do not isolate yourself while on the motherhood express.

Forgive yourself for the unrealistic expectations you had set for yourself before you had the baby and set new realistic goals. If you had previously thought you'd go back to size zero after only a few weeks only to find yourself having added more weight, forgive yourself, and start walking. Incorporate your baby in your exercise by taking along their stroller during your evening walks. Be easy on yourself if you have ordered takeout dinner more days than you made a home meal. You're a new mother with a new baby, and things will take time before they are "perfect".

Keep in mind all the physical problems that you might experience post-delivery and seek help on how to manage them. Women who have given birth are likely to experience constipation, incontinence, hemorrhoids, and sore breasts. Constipation after delivery can be caused by several factors. If you have a C-section, constipation could be brought on by the fact that you underwent major surgery and the digestive system needs time to recover. Pain relievers administered during labor can also slow down the digestive tract. A sore perineum can also scare a new mother from making a bowel movement if they fear tearing their episiotomy stitches. Whether your constipation is caused by physiological or psychological factors, you can relieve the problem by eating high-fiber foods coupled with drinking plenty of water. Do not ignore the urge to do as holding back only makes the stool harder which makes it more painful to pass.

Urinary incontinence after birth is common, especially in women who have delivered vaginally. Urinary incontinence happens when the muscles and ligaments that support the urethra are stretched during labor and delivery, thus easily allowing urine to leak out. Urinary incontinence usually resolves within a year of delivery. Kegel exercises and lifestyle changes can help you regain control of your bladder. In severe cases of incontinence, there might be a need for medical intervention including electrical stimulation therapy and surgery.

Returning to work after birth is another topic that first-time moms should pay attention to as they consider their post-partum recovery. Your first day back at work might be wrought with anxiety, worry, restlessness, and even depression. Some employers are very supportive of returning moms, while others aren't. If your employer falls in the latter category, make sure of the benefits offered to returning moms to make your transition easier. Flexible working hours, for instance, come in handy when a mom needs to feed their baby first before reporting to work. If your employer is not keen to make allowances for you, make sure you have a solid child-care plan back home. Alternatively, consider changing employers and going for a job that supports the social development of their employees. Whatever decision you make, keep in mind that you are protected by the employment and labor laws of the region you work in.

Chapter 14:
Detrimental Mistakes to Avoid During Pregnancy

So, you're pregnant with your first child and wholesomely excited about this journey. You're also terrified because well-meaning friends and family have laid bare all the gruesome details of pregnancies, labor, and delivery. To get prepared for your bundle of joy and your new role as a mother, you have read all the pregnancy books you could lay your hands on. You still do not feel ready. You fear that one wrong move will end up in disaster. While you had initially planned on enjoying your pregnancy to the fullest, you are finding yourself battling nerves and anxiety continually. What to do?

This chapter outlines the top mistakes that you should avoid during pregnancy. Once you have these committed to memory, avoiding them should be easy. You can after that look forward to enjoying the incredible journey that is bringing a human being into this world.

Indulging in Alcohol
Most expecting moms know that they are not supposed to indulge in alcohol while pregnant. What some moms do not know is that there are plenty of products that have alcoholic content that you might be

using unknowingly. Such products include mouthwash, flavored extracts, nail polish remover, aftershave, perfume, and even some bug sprays. To avoid inadvertently interacting with alcohol, always read the ingredients label of the product that you purchase. After having your baby, avoid indulging in too much alcohol especially if you are breastfeeding.

Too Much Coffee

While you might like your cup of coffee, you'll need to cut back on the caffeine once you find out that you are expecting. Doctors recommend reducing the daily intake of caffeine to 200 milligrams, which is what you'll find in a regular cup of coffee. Caffeine can also be found in black and green tea, so you'll need to watch out for those as well. During the first few months of pregnancy, caffeine can make your morning sickness even worse. It is yet another reason why you need to go slow on the caffeine.

Type of Food and Portions

While you may be 'eating for two', it is important that you ensure you are eating the right food and the right portions. Eating everything in sight, junk food included, is not the proper way to go about your pregnancy diet. While you might feel the need to indulge your cravings, ensure that you are keeping a healthy balance between what is needed by the baby and what you need. Discussing your diet options with your doctor is a great way to approach your food habits during this period. Also, if it's fatty, spicy, raw, or questionable, forego it until after the baby is born.

Attitude Towards Pregnancy

There are several things about you and your life that will change when you become pregnant. You might have to avoid certain foods, increase your vitamins intake, and maybe say goodbye to contact sports for a while. You should not treat pregnancy as a condition or sickness. While you need to be more careful, it does not mean that your life must come to an end. Pregnant women can, and should, carry on with their lives as they have done before. You should still be able to go to work, engage in your hobbies, go for that shopping spree, cook your favorite meals, and hang out with your friends as you have done before. At the same time, you should remember that the rules that applied before you were pregnant still apply. If it wasn't a good idea before you were expecting, it still is not a good idea after finding out you are pregnant.

Avoiding sex

Some women will experience a heightened sex drive when they are pregnant. On the other hand, some women will completely wipe out sex from their schedule. Unless your doctor warns you against sexual activity, it is necessary to continue being intimate with your partner. Sex during pregnancy has excellent benefits which include improved blood circulation. It also increases bonding with your partner and boosts your self-confidence. In the later stages of pregnancy, sex can help induce labor. This is because the prostaglandins contained in the semen can soften the cervix and pelvic muscles and aid in contractions. If you start to feel uncomfortable during sex as the bump grows, switch positions and find one that works best for you. Stay open and honest so that your partner is on board with ensuring your comfort comes first.

Lack of Sleep

Even though you have a busy lifestyle with a million things to do, it is essential to get enough sleep. Getting enough rest ensures that your body gets the rest it needs to recuperate from all the heavy lifting of growing a human being. It is recommended that pregnant women get at least ten hours of sleep every night. Some pregnant women will completely neglect rest, which is detrimental both to you and your developing baby. If you're having trouble sleeping, refer to Chapter 5: Sleeping the Right Way for tips and tricks on how to make bedtime easier for you and your growing bump. Remember that you do not have to sleep only at night. You can reduce your sleep deficit by stealing small naps during the day.

Too Many Vitamins and Supplements

You might be feeling excited about getting all the necessary vitamins and supplements for your baby, but don't overdo it. Your baby's primary source of nutrition should ideally be the whole, healthy foods that you consume. The vitamins and supplements are intended to supplement your everyday diet and not replace it. Don't avoid vitamins, but don't depend on them either. If in doubt regarding where to draw the line, consult with your doctor. If you have been taking prenatal vitamins before you got pregnant, consult with your doctor so that you know whether you should keep taking them. Too much of anything is harmful, and this applies to prenatal vitamins also. Your doctor might recommend taking specific vitamins and supplements for only a few months of the pregnancy. This is fine as they'll usually have a good reason for recommending this.

Too Much Sun

Sunbathing is fantastic and all but not so much when you are pregnant. Expecting moms tend to have more sensitive skins. As such, you should take great precaution to avoid the dangerous effects of too much exposure to direct sunlight. Wear enough sunscreen for protection, stay in the shade, and drink enough water for hydration. Too much sun can cause heatstroke which is terrible for the baby. Overheating is the same reason why some schools of thought tell moms not to soak in hot baths for an extended period. Your baby can regulate their temperature only after they are born and not immediately so. While they are in the womb, your baby depends on you to make wise decisions about when to bask in the sun and when to stay in the shade. If you experience overheating while in the house or outside going about your work, try sucking on an ice lolly or placing a cold compress behind your neck.

Socializing with Sick People

While you might love your aunty dearly, you might also want to wait until she overcomes her nasty chickenpox before hugging her too tightly. Pregnancy is a sensitive period, and your immune system is usually running at less than optimum ability. Do yourself a favor and avoid sick people to avoid getting sick yourself. Even if you have obtained the necessary vaccines, exercise discretion and caution. Speaking of vaccines, you'll probably want to read up on the vaccines that are necessary for expecting moms and newborns. Staying informed will help you make informed choices for your baby and for yourself too.

Stressing Over Everything

In life, even the best-laid plans come with flaws and deviations. Things will most definitely not always go according to plan when you're pregnant either. While pregnant, you're hormonal and emotional, and it can be easy to get carried away by everyday stresses. Do not make the mistake of being so caught in the hassles of life that you forget to enjoy the journey you are undertaking and the miracle that you are creating. When you start to feel overwhelmed, stop and exhale. Stop and ask for help. Stop and have some chamomile tea. Stop and nap. It is highly advisable that you remain aware of your breaking points and ensure you do not get there. If you have experienced depression in the past or any other mental illness, talk to your doctor so that you know what help is available for you.

Obsessing Over Your Image

You're pregnant. Your body is literally manufacturing a human being inside of you. Most people do not expect you to look like a Victoria Secret's model during this period of your life. Embrace the way your body is changing without feeling ashamed of it. A lot of pregnant women make the mistake of hiding their blossoming bump under layers and layers of frumpy clothing. Do not fall into the trap of demanding perfection from yourself just because you have been fed the same by media outlets and the likes. While pregnant, you are only required to stay healthy, take care of yourself, and feel good about yourself. Your stretch marks should be worn loud and proud. Get some nice well-fitting clothes and enjoy all the thrills and frills of maternity fashion. You deserve it.

Making the Announcement Too Soon

After finding out that you are pregnant, allow yourself and your partner to digest the information before sharing it with everyone else. Walk around with the knowledge that your love has brought forth a new person, without inviting anyone else to share the secret. There is really no pressure to share this information with everyone else, and especially not your friends and followers on social media. And when you are genuinely comfortable sharing this information, you can make your grand announcement from the rooftops. Typically, couples will wait until eight weeks before announcing because then the risk of miscarriage is expected to have reduced. Still, no rule says you cannot wait longer.

Being Crippled by Your Fears
It is normal and natural to have great fears during pregnancy, especially when not-so-nice circumstances are surrounding you. If you have experienced miscarriage before, it is natural to fear the same happening again. If you have tried to conceive for the longest time before finally falling pregnant, it is normal to feel apprehensive about the pregnancy. If you are going through pregnancy alone, it is entirely human to feel scared out of your wits. Do not let the fear overcome you. There has been a lot of stigmas associated with matters of pregnancy in the past. Things are getting better now, and there are a lot more people willing to listen. Find one of those and open. Pregnancy is an extraordinary journey, and you should never allow your fears to stop you from enjoying it. And remember, just because you do not feel like it does not mean you'll not be a badass, kick-ass momma. You've got this figured out way more than you think you do. Whatever you haven't figured out, you've got the rest of your life (or at least eighteen years) to do so!

Too Much Planning or Not Enough Planning
You can plan the perfect birth plan for the entire nine months of your pregnancy and still be caught flat-footed on the day of the delivery. The best way to ensure you enjoy your pregnancy, through to labor and delivery, is to prepare for the essentials without obsessing over details. Your baby will not necessarily dance to the tunes outlined in your birth plan, and you can bet something will go wrong somewhere.

Instead of playing out the perfect birth over and over in your mind, prepare your mind and body for the honor of giving birth. Exercise, eat well and meditate. Take childbirth classes that teach you the practicality of giving birth.

On the other hand, winging it during pregnancy will just not cut it. Even if you are not keen on planning, iron out the necessary details of labor and delivery before you go into the delivery room. Choose a doctor you trust, get your insurance in order, enlist the help of a birth partner, prepare yourself mentally, and prepare the nursery for your baby's homecoming. Even having a rough plan is better than not having a plan at all.

Not Attending Childbirth Classes

Childbirth classes are a useful tool to make use of during a first-time pregnancy because they teach you things nobody else has taught you before. While mothers and daughters tend to discuss a whole lot of things, it's unlikely that your mom has taught you how to breathe correctly during labor. It is important to be confident in your ability to deliver without someone needing to give a PowerPoint presentation of how it's done. On the same note, it is important to appreciate that as a first-time mom, there are a lot of things you do now know yet. Childbirth classes teach you these things so that you are aware of what to expect and what to do when things do not go as expected.

Playing Doctor

Pregnancy is not a time to self-medicate. Just because a certain page on the Internet said you're suffering from a disease doesn't mean you should rush and buy the medicine. Never self-medicate during pregnancy. Always consult with your doctor. Some medicines that were safe for you before pregnancy could have detrimental effects on your unborn baby. If you are dealing with aches and pains, ask a doctor to recommend a safe painkiller that you'll use throughout the pregnancy. Alternatively, consider relieving your pains in other ways instead of rushing for a pill. For example, instead of treating your headache with pain relievers, try addressing the root cause of the headache. This could be dehydration or even stress. Drink enough water and take it easy, and you are likely to suffer fewer headaches.

Keeping the Wrong Company

That friend that encourages you to drink while pregnant and doesn't believe in the dangers of smoking is not a good friend to keep around when pregnant. Your friend from work who tells you it's okay to stay up partying all night while you are six-months pregnant is lying. You will be required to stay conscious of who in your circle means well for you and who doesn't. After your baby arrives, this will be even more important as you do not want them to grow up in a toxic environment. Sometimes, in some very unfortunate circumstances, this means keeping a distance from your baby's father until you are ready to deal with them in an empowered manner. Life is not easy, and it doesn't get easier during pregnancy. However, you are not powerless, and you can control some things in your life.

Chapter 15:
Top Pregnancy Tips and Essentials

Pregnancy is a beautiful adventure that is experienced by a woman, their partner, and loved ones, and the miracle they are carrying within them. While all pregnancies involve the conception and development of a human being within the loving and haven that is a womb, every woman experience pregnancy differently. Certain things have been tried and tested and found to be true for most pregnancies. In this final chapter, you'll find top pregnancy tips and essentials that will come in handy during your nine-month rollercoaster.

Maternity Fashion

At some point in your pregnancy, your go-to jeans stop being your go-to jeans. The lovely dress that you wore at every occasion takes a back seat, and all your nice tops seem like a joke now. This is because your bump has grown, and nothing fits anymore. During the entire first trimester and part of the second trimester, you can get away with sticking with your pre-pregnancy wardrobe. However, at around the seventh month, you'll have to change to a more pregnancy-friendly wardrobe. Maternity jeans, leggings and maternity bras are just some of the essentials that you need to have. Maternity bras are especially important in ensuring your breasts stay supported during this period when they are becoming fuller and heavier. When choosing maternity bras, do not go for bras with underwire. Underwired bras can squeeze the breasts awkwardly, and make you feel uncomfortable. The last thing you need is something to inhibit the comfort of your breasts which are now fuller and tender in readiness for nursing. Remember that maternity fashion does not need to be boring. You can have fun with colors and prints. Whenever possible, go for items of clothing that you can wear even after you deliver your baby. When all is said and done, the best maternity fashion is whatever makes you feel comfortable and good about yourself.

Childbirth Classes

As a first-time mom, you'll need all the information you can get about pregnancy and childbirth. Hopefully, this book has answered most if not all the questions that you have about pregnancy and childbirth. Consider supplementing the information in this book with some practical childbirth classes. There are different types of childbirth education classes including Lamaze classes, Bradley Method classes, and Hypnobirthing classes. The Bradley Method classes teach that childbirth is a task that female bodies were designed for and that, with the right preparation, women can go through birth without suffering. Lamaze classes teach women to trust their intuition during childbirth and empowers them to make informed decisions about their healthcare, when pregnant and beyond. Childbirth classes can be attended on your own or with your birth partner. It is ideal to have your birth partner with you so that they can use the skills and techniques learned in class to support you during childbirth.

Essential Oils

During your pregnancy, essential oils are going to come in handy in several ways. At the onset of your pregnancy, you are likely to experience lots of morning sickness. Lavender, peppermint, ginger, and chamomile will help you feel a whole lot better. These essential oils can make you feel better even when you're not pregnant! Pour a drop of any of these oils on a cotton ball and sniff away. Alternatively, just inhale directly from the bottom. You could also leave open bottles of essential oils strategically placed in your bedroom or living room area so you can inhale the essence all day.

As your pregnancy progresses, especially in the third trimester, you'll find that your vaginal and perineal area might become irritated and puffy. You might end up feeling uncomfortable and even itchy. To prevent this from happening, use cypress, geranium, and lavender to soothe this area. Just pour a drop of each in the palm of your hand and mix together and then apply to your lady parts. An alternative to the coconut oil is olive oil. Taking care of your southern bits during pregnancy will help them recover well from the exertion that is childbirth.

Essential oils also come in handy when it comes to helping you fall asleep better. Pregnancy comes with many surprises, and one of those might be difficulty falling asleep. Chamomile and lavender are exceptionally useful in helping you fall asleep during those nights when insomnia kicks in. Some calming essential oils can also be used during the process of labor to relax the mom-to-be. These oils should be used in collaboration with the relaxation techniques learned during childbirth classes.

Mental Health

The changes, both physical and physiological, that take place in your body can overwhelm your mind during pregnancy. It is critical that you remain aware of the state of your mental health during pregnancy. It is common for women to experience depression and anxiety during pregnancy. For women who have a history of mental illness, discontinuing intake of medication for the sake of the baby can have a detrimental effect on the mom's well-being. Keep the lines of communication with your doctor open during pregnancy so that they can jump in and assist for instance by recommending a therapist when needed. If you are lucky enough to have one, make use of your support system. Meditate. Go for yoga. Take long walks and breaks when you need them. Nobody said that you must achieve everything in one day. Pregnancy is a nine-month journey, but a whole lot of it is taking each day as it comes.

Constipation

Constipation affects a lot of women during pregnancy. Constipation can lead to swollen hemorrhoids, which tend to be very painful. Swollen hemorrhoids develop in the anal area when a lot of pressure is applied to the area, which is typical when you are struggling to have a bowel movement. The best way to deal with constipation is to avoid it before it happens. Immediately after finding out that you that you are pregnant, ensure your diet is high in fiber and stay hydrated by drinking enough water. Whole grains and dark leafy vegetables are examples of foods that are high in fiber content.

If you've had a C-section, the pain that comes with making a bowel movement can put you off from going to the toilet when you need it. Put aside this fear and power through your bowel movement because if you don't, you'll get constipated, which is even more painful. Contact your doctor if your constipation is coupled with rectal bleeding as this might indicate a bigger problem.

Intimacy

After your baby is born, you might not have the time or energy to spend a whole lot of romantic time with your partner. The pregnancy period is your last chance to enjoy some alone time with your partner without worrying about the baby. Some women tend to shy away from sexual intimacy during pregnancy since they're worried about how they look or because they feel uncomfortable. Some are even worried that sex might hurt the baby. Your baby is well protected in the uterus by the amniotic sac and will not be bothered by a little lovemaking.

Unless your doctor advises otherwise, it is safe to continue being intimate with your partner. Intimacy can also be spending time without getting physical. After the kids, it becomes harder to be spontaneous. Make the best of the pregnancy period to schedule intimate and spontaneous getaways with your man.

Memories

You will only ever be pregnant with your first baby once, so make sure you take enough photos to last you a lifetime. Immortalize your pregnancy journey by hiring a good photographer who will give you professional shots that you'll be proud of. If you are not up to hiring someone, just take the photos yourself. Thankfully, you only need a smartphone with a high-resolution camera to take all the photos that you want. Pictures are great for looking back on and even sharing with the baby once they're old enough to appreciate what you went through to bring them to this earth.

Prenatal Vitamins

Prenatal vitamins are taken to help cover the nutritional gaps that exist in the diet of a mom-to-be. They do not help you get pregnant, but they help the body to be ready to nurture a baby once you become pregnant. Prenatal vitamins supply the body with vitamins and minerals such as the B vitamins, vitamin D, iron, folic acid, and even calcium. It is best to start taking prenatal vitamins at least three months before conception. Women who do not intend to get pregnant should not take prenatal vitamins as prolonged use could lead to accumulation to toxic levels.

Vaccinations

Over the years, vaccines have become a controversial topic with some groups of thought informally referred to as "anti-vaxxers" campaigning vehemently against vaccinations. As a first-time mom, it is essential to get all the information first before making a decision that could potentially harm your child and even put their life at risk. At a fundamental level, it is essential to understand how a vaccine works. A vaccine is administered to stimulate the immune system so that the body can develop defenses to attack a pathogen should that pathogen manifest in the body later.

Vaccines are used to prevent certain diseases. The intended end goal for vaccines is to achieve herd immunity and eliminate certain diseases. So far, only smallpox has been eradicated through vaccination. It is hoped that other diseases such as polio and measles can soon follow suit. While pregnant, you'll receive some vaccines to protect yourself and especially the baby. After the baby is born, they will require vaccines too. Common vaccines administered to babies after birth include the chickenpox vaccines, hepatitis, measles, and meningitis.

Hospital Bag

Catherine Emily

A hospital bag is a bag, suitcase, or trunk-full of items that you carry with you when going to the hospital to give birth. You should pack your hospital bag when you are 37 or 38 weeks pregnant, or earlier if you anticipate labor to begin before your due date. The items that you pack in your hospital bag can make all the difference between having a comfortable stay in the hospital and having an awful one. Usually, the items that you'll pack are what is required for the birth and what is needed after birth. Make a checklist of all the items that you require to make sure you do not forget to pack anything. Some things that you'll need to include in your hospital bag are:

- Mandatory documents such as insurance and identification cards

- Comfortable wear that you're okay staining, including socks, a warm sweater or robe, and clothes for going home

- Phone and charger for you and your partner so you can keep family updated

- Relaxation material such as your favorite music or magazines to pass the time with

- A receiving blanket for baby and other warm blankets for the ride home

Expecting First Time Moms

- A warm set of clothes for baby; your partner or a trusted friend can bring more sets during visits

- Travel-size toiletries including shampoo, lotion, toothpaste, deodorant, and a hairbrush for you and your partner because it gets sweaty, and you'll need to clean up

- Eyeglasses or contact lenses if you wear them to see your bundle of joy when they are finally delivered

- A nightgown that you can easily say goodbye to when it gets ruined

- Maternity underwear if you do not want to wear the hospital-issued underwear

- Your favorite pillow so that you can get as comfortable as you possibly can during labor

- A breastfeeding pillow so that you can comfortably breastfeed your baby after they arrive

- An infant seat for the journey home; if you forget this, you will not be allowed to take the baby home

- A change of clothes for your partner who has been working so hard to cheer you through labor

- A camera and charger, if possible, with back-up power and memory, to capture all the important moments

Breastfeeding

It is usually recommended that breastfeeding should begin immediately after birth or as soon as the baby and mom are stable. Newborns are typically able to latch onto a breast immediately after birth, although some require some pushing. When a newborn is placed in their mother's arms, they instinctively start to seek the breast. This is because they learned how to suckle while still in the womb, often practicing on their own thumbs, and are ready to get started on the real thing.

For the first few moments when you start breastfeeding, you might experience soreness in your nipples which can be very painful. You might even experience cracked or bleeding nipples, a condition which can be excruciating and even put you off breastfeeding. Usually, it's okay to keep breastfeeding your baby even if your nipples are cracked or bleeding. There are some measures you can take to alleviate the pain. One of them is applying a moisturizing cream or cold compress and using hydrogel pads to soothe your sore nipples.

It is common for a breastfeeding mom's breasts to become engorged when they are full of milk. When this happens, you might feel a lot of pain which is only relieved when the baby feeds or some of the milk is let out of the breast. As a first-time mom, it is necessary to be aware of the difference between normal engorgement caused by too much milk and mastitis, which is a more severe and painful condition. Mastitis occurs when bacteria enters the breast or when a milk duct becomes blocked. Signs of mastitis include breast pain and swelling, fever, and red blotches on your skin. Your breasts might also feel hot to the touch, and you might notice some lumps. If you suspect you have mastitis, get in touch with your doctor. This condition is usually solved with antibiotics in the case of a bacterial infection and usually resolves within a few days. In severe cases, there might be a need for incision and drainage.

While breastfeeding is a great way to provide nourishment to your child while bonding with them, consider introducing a bottle later so that your partner can relieve you of night feeding duties. Training your baby to use a bottle will also come in handy when you resume work as someone else can feed them while you are away. Exclusively bottle-feeding your baby is fine too and has no bearing on the sort of person they will become once they grow up. With bottle-feeding, you'll need to ensure that the bottles are properly cleaned and kept sterile so that your baby is not at risk of falling ill.

Home Birth Vs. Hospital Birth

As an expecting mom, you can choose to give birth at a hospital or in your home. Pregnant women prefer to give birth at home for various reasons, a top one being that the familiar surroundings of home can be relaxing during labor. If your doctor or midwife gives the okay, you can comfortably give birth at home, surrounded by family if you so wish. Home births are usually less costly than hospital birth and tend to be devoid of the pressure to use medications. They are also more convenient as you do not need to travel to the hospital when labor begins. You'll tend to feel more comfortable giving birth at home, especially if you fear hospitals. You can also indulge in your religious or cultural practices much better at home as this is your safe space. On the flipside, home births tend to be messy. You might also require urgent medical intervention, which will mean being rushed to the hospital in the middle of labor.

A hospital birth, on the other hand, is statistically safer and should be the only option for women with high-risk pregnancies. You will also have a larger medical team at your disposal when you give birth in a hospital. Even at a hospital, your views are listened to. If you do not want pain medication, nobody will force it down your throat. You should not be discouraged from giving birth in a hospital just because you are fearful.

Embarrassing Moments of Childbirth
You may have heard it before and cringed inwardly, but it is true-it is normal to have a bowel movement during childbirth. This information is probably the last thing a first-time mom wants to hear. Just thinking of going number two while everyone peeks at your nether regions is enough to make you swear off childbirth for the rest of your life. The good news is that your medical team will have experienced these

Expecting First Time Moms

numerous times before and will most likely keep experiencing it after you've delivered and gone home. Your doctors and nurses are prepared for the messes of childbirth, and you can bet nobody will bat an eyelid when your bowels refuse to cooperate.

Hopefully, your confidence as a first-time mom-to-be is higher now than it was when you started reading this book. It is normal for new moms to experience angst about pregnancy and motherhood. A few months with your baby are all you will need to realize that you are well-suited for this honorable role, regardless of how you might feel on some days. Keep in mind too that billions of women have walked this journey that you are about to walk and successfully so. You, like the rest of them, will be just fine.

Mindful Pregnancy for New Moms

The Ultimate Guide for The First Year, What to Expect for Each Trimester, Hypnobirthing, Childbirth, Breastfeeding, And the Secrets No One Tells You

Chapter 1:
Things I Wish I Knew While Pregnant

The journey of pregnancy is fun, exciting, stressful, and joyful. There's so much to learn during these nine months, and while the journey is something you will always fondly remember, there are going to be times when you wish somebody told you what you were going to experience during these nine months and how you'll feel.

There were so many things I wish I knew during my first pregnancy, so I decided to share this information with you to make your life a little easier. These nine months mark the beginning of a new chapter in your life and the more prepared you are, the better you'll be able to handle it.

Don't Stress About Your Marriage

A lot of pregnant friends tell me they are worried about pregnancy because of the distance they must maintain from their husbands or partners for the first three months. You are most likely going to lose interest in sex during your first trimester, and most women fear their partners may not take it too well.

Honestly, men are just as excited to become fathers, and they are ready to make sacrifices for the well-being of their baby. You'll be surprised how helpful and intimate your partner gets, even though there is no sex during the first trimester. If you're worried about things changing once the baby arrives, don't! I watched my husband transform from a childish boy to a responsible man the minute he held my baby in the delivery room.

If a man truly loves you, he will stick by you through thick and thin, and pregnancy is one of the most cherished moments in a relationship which he is going to enjoy just as much as you do.

Don't shy away from sharing facts about your pregnancy with your husband or partner, make them a part of it and you'll enjoy the journey as a couple.

You Will Get A Chance to Relax!

Ok, I'm going to be honest with you, this might not be exactly post-delivery or for a few months after, but soon enough your baby is going to sleep for long hours, and you're going to rest. A lot of women stress because they say they won't be able to keep up with the feeding demands of a baby. Trust me—once the maternal instincts kick in, all you'll care about is for your baby to have a full tummy and be well rested. The first few months may be stressful, but they are the most beautiful months of your life and watching your little baby grow, is something you will look forward to! Each time you place your baby on the weighing scale, and you see an increase in weight you'll have a proud smile on your face.

Educate Yourself About What Happens After Pregnancy

There's a lot of information out there with regards to how you should prepare for your pregnancy and what you need to do in order to have a healthy one, but there are very few people who to talk about what happens after labor.

Let me say this, labor isn't a cakewalk, and neither are the few days after. Whether you have a vaginal birth, or you opted for C-section, you will have stitches, and stitches take time to heal.

While a vaginal birth may be easier to deal with because you don't need to worry about holding or nursing your baby, you are going to have trouble when you want to pee.

A C-section will be a little tougher for you to deal with because your stitches will hurt, and breastfeeding could be challenging.

Breastfeeding may look simply, but it is something you need time to get used to. Prepare yourself for sore nipples for the initial few weeks.

A quick tip before you get into the hospital - Carry soft cotton clothes that don't stick to your body to wear on your way back from the hospital. If you're investing in nursing bras, make sure they are soft cotton nursing bras that will not irritate sore skin.

You Don't Need Too Many Things

Don't spend money on unnecessary things your baby is going to outgrow, instead look for things that are practical, cost-effective and come in handy. The most important thing you need are diapers, wet wipes, and full breasts! Don't buy too many clothes! Infants grow fast, and they will outgrow these clothes a lot faster than you think. The 0 to 3-month size lasted my baby barely month! We had so many clothes gifted to us we didn't get a chance to use them all.

If you are throwing a baby shower, have a gift registry and let people know what you need, so these things come handy. If you can ask for a breast pump, do it! It's so convenient on-the-go, and you can travel with your baby comfortably. You can even plan an outing without having to worry about nursing.

You Need A Body Pillow

Sleeping during pregnancy is one of the hardest things to do, especially if you love sleeping on your stomach. I struggled a lot because I love sleeping on my stomach and I just couldn't get myself to sleep if I couldn't get into that position. This was until I discovered the body pillow. The body pillow helped me sleep comfortably through my pregnancy, and it also gave me an illusion that I was sleeping on my stomach. The pillow also acts as a defense mechanism and prevents you from putting too much weight on your stomach while you sleep. The worst part about the body pillow is I cannot give it up even after I have delivered.

Heartburn Remedies

If this is your first pregnancy you are bound to be nervous and you would do everything in your power to enhance your comfort level and keep your baby safe. My husband went crazy whenever I'd suffer from heartburn, and he would make sure I could on the best antacid tablets available at the drugstore.

One day I happened to come across an antacid liquid bottle and decided to try it out. I couldn't see my husband going crazy looking for the antacid tablets each week. As it turned out the antacid liquid worked perfectly, and it cured my heartburn instantly.

Quick tip - Trust your gut and do not opt for overly expensive products, unless recommended by the doctor.

Do Not Get Frustrated

It is very common for you to get frustrated within the first couple of months of pregnancy. It's a journey, and there are times you want the nine months to go by quickly. If such feelings creep in, you should focus on the fact that you are part of a miracle. A new life growing inside you is an amazing experience, and you should keep reminding yourself that you are part of it.

Stay Active

This is one thing I made sure I did during my pregnancy term. Giving birth is a difficult physical experience, and you need to be in good shape, or it will take a toll on you.

There are various ways you can stay fit. You could try yoga, or you could go for a walk daily or even ride a bike if your doctor says it's fine. You need to realize that your body is changing and not staying active will make the transition process tougher. Continue with your normal life until the third trimester, and make sure you do not succumb to the physical exertion pregnancy brings along with it.

Remember, while it's good to stay fit and exercise regularly, always consult your doctor before choosing an activity. While it's rare, some women are advised bed rest during their pregnancy.

Spend A Lot of Time Enjoy Yourself

While this is easier said than done, you need to keep taking a break from stressing about pregnancy all the time and just be you.

You need to continue living your social life and make sure you have a lot of fun with your friends and family members. This will help lift your spirits, and your mindset will be positive and happy during your pregnancy. Do everything you loved doing; however, stay within the boundaries and do not let it harm your child.

Chapter 2:
Get Your Pregnancy Off to A Good Start

Pregnancy is a massive responsibility on your shoulders. You need to take care of yourself as well as the health of your child. From the day you learn you're pregnant, you need to make sure you focus on a healthy pregnancy. The only way you would be able to do that is if you take care of your health. There are various other benefits of leading a healthy lifestyle, and I will talk about those benefits later in the book. You need to take care of your well-being, and it all begins with the first trimester. Here are a few things you need to do in order to get your pregnancy off to a good start.

Prenatal Care

You need to enroll for prenatal care and consult your doctor as soon as you learn you're pregnant. Look for non-invasive prenatal tests or NIPT to make sure your pregnancy is healthy. NIPT helps in detecting Patau syndrome, Edward's syndrome, and Down's syndrome. Initially, NIPT was recommended only for women above a certain age because they were considered high risk. However, these days the NIPT is recommended for all pregnant women.

Stay Healthy During Your Pregnancy

It's important for you to make sure you stay healthy during your pregnancy if you want a healthy baby. There are few things you can and cannot eat so educate yourself with regards to what you should and shouldn't include in your diet. Smoking and drinking are something you must let go of, and this includes second-hand smoking. If your partner smokes, you need to convince him to quit or not smoke when he is around you. Avoid bending as much as possible because this is not healthy to your baby.

Take Prenatal Vitamins

There are several vitamins you need to take when you're pregnant. Make sure you take all of these on time and on a regular basis. Folic acid is vital, and it is something you must carry on for at least the first three months depending on what your doctor suggests. I started taking Folic acid even before I was pregnant. I also had Calcium and Iron supplements during my pregnancy to help with better fetal development.

Exercise

Exercising is important during pregnancy unless advised otherwise. Not only does it help keep your body active, but it changes your mood. The best part about being pregnant in today's date is you will find tons of pregnancy classes around you, and you should enroll in them. These classes are specifically designed for pregnant women and help them stay fit and active during the nine months of pregnancy while taking precautions for the baby. I did yoga until my eighth month of pregnancy to stay healthy, and this worked wonders during my delivery because it helped me stay relaxed and calm through the pain.

When you're pregnant, always look out for signs your body gives out and if you can't handle any exercise or if you find it difficult to do, don't push yourself too much. It's important to move but not to the extent that you put strain on your baby or on your body.

Plan Birthing in Advance

Some women prefer a vaginal birth without any assisted procedures while others choose an epidural or even schedule a C-section. There is nothing wrong with any method of delivery you choose if you are confident about it. Consult your doctor and ask them about the pros and cons of the various delivery options you can pick from. You should also discuss with your partner whether they would like to be present during the delivery. I had my husband with me throughout my labor. While most women want their husband with them during delivery, some might not be comfortable with their husbands being around.

If you are not comfortable wearing hospital clothes, make sure you talk to your doctor in advance and inform them about what you would like to wear. Educate yourself with regards to the various complications that might arise and how to deal with it.

Educate Yourself

You probably have heard many women tell you different stories about what they experienced during labor but is always better for you to experience it the first hand. If you can get your hands-on birthing videos, you may want to check them out just so you know what you are getting into. I am not saying it isn't painful, because it is. But it is not something you can't handle, and when the time comes, you will get all the power to push your baby and bring him or her into this world. The more you learn about delivery and post-delivery, the more it is going to benefit you because you will handle your pregnancy better and with more confidence.

Kegels Is Your Friend

Kegels exercises help to strengthen your pelvic muscles and help you control your bladder. It's great for your uterus especially when your baby is growing in it. Kegel exercises makes your pregnancy much easier, and it helps to uterus adjust with the changes more conveniently. I practiced Kegels throughout my pregnancy, and I still do it! It's a great way to help your uterus get back to normal after delivery. Here is how it's done.

- Try holding back your urine and then release.

- Hold for another 3 seconds then release and then for another 3 seconds and then release.

- Repeat this process a total of 10 times in one go.

Do this as many times as possible during the day because it's beneficial. It's better to do it when you are sitting as it applies more pressure and it makes your pelvic muscles stronger.

Change Your Chores

The tasks you do on a regular basis may need to change once you are pregnant. Exposure to toxic chemicals such as bathroom cleaning agents and acid is something you need to stay away from. You also need to avoid heavy lifting so those trips to the grocery market may need to decrease or you'll have to be accompanied by someone every time you go. Never ever get on a step stool or on a ladder when you are pregnant as this can be very dangerous.

You also must make it a habit to sit as often as possible. Standing for long durations is not good for your baby. Bending is also not recommended, so try to keep anything that you need at a higher level. Try to avoid using the bathtub when you are pregnant especially during the later months. I remember going out for a holiday with my husband and not being able to get out of the bathtub because I was too scared it would be slippery and I may fall.

Track Your Weight

You can't afford to stay in shape when you are pregnant, and you must gain weight. A healthy weight gain is anywhere between 25 and 35 pounds. Anything above that is usually overweight, and anything below is considered underweight. Calculate your ideal weight and try attaining that weight in order to stay healthy.

Invest in Good Shoes

Trust me when I say this, you need the best possible pair of shoes when you are pregnant. Forget those dazzling slim pairs you enjoy wearing and look for something comforting. Let's not forget, you need to stay off heels when you're pregnant. You can also switch to therapeutic slippers because these can help you feel comforted and relaxed.

Get Regular Massages

Make sure you comfort yourself as much as possible when you are pregnant, and this involves therapeutic spa treatments as well. Remember, you can't get into a hot tub or a sauna that's too warm. The massages should be relaxing. Look for something that involves a calming and soothing oil to help relax you. Don't go in for painful massages during your pregnancy. Look for ones that help your body feel energized and revitalized.

Indulge in The Things You Love

If you think you're busy being pregnant, wait until the baby comes. If you want to make sure you stay relaxed during your pregnancy you should go ahead and do the things you feel you may miss out on once your baby is here.

Try sleeping for a minimum of 8 hours every night. If your sleep is not regular, then you need to make sure you consult your doctor for remedies. Listen to a lot of soothing music to help calm your nerves and go for long walks in the evening along with your partner. Do things you enjoy, such as getting a manicure or going for a fun dinner with your girl gang. The reason you need to indulge during your pregnancy is you should have no regrets about missing out when the baby is here. FOMO (fear of missing out) is a major issue these days and can get people depressed.

Consult Your Doctor Regularly

If it's your first pregnancy, there will be a lot of bodily changes that may confuse you. There are lots of twitches and aches you will feel during your first term, and you need to make sure all of these are normal. If this is your second pregnancy and you are experiencing something new, that is also a good reason for you to dial your doctor's number. Some of the things you should be concerned about include:

- Severe pain in the back

- Strong cramps at different times of the day

- Painting as well as dizziness

- Vaginal discharge

- Palpitations

- Breathing difficulty

- Constant vomiting

- Very little baby activity

- Swelling of the joints

If you have experienced any of these problems or you are experiencing something new, make sure you contact your doctor as soon as possible.

Travel Carefully

Flying is usually a tricky situation for most pregnant women. The best times to fly are different for different women, and you need to consult your doctor before you take off to for a weekend trip or to visit your relatives for a few weeks.

Ideally, the weeks between 14 and 28 are safest to fly, but no travel plan should be made without checking for two things - the approval of your doctor as well as airline restrictions. If you are cleared to fly, make sure you stock up on a lot of water, so you stay hydrated during the flight. If it is a long flight, make sure that you get up and take a walk every half an hour or so to make sure that there are no blood clots forming. Always opt for an aisle seat. This will give you more room to sit, and it will also make it easier to go to the bathroom and walk around when needed.

Rely on Sunscreen

When I was pregnant, the one thing I realized was my skin was very sensitive. This made me prone to dark patches, sunburn and spots appearing on my face. The one thing I did was apply sunscreen with SPF of 30 or even higher. I always look for creams which were chemical free. Apart from sunscreen I also made sure I always wore sunglasses and a hat. No one told me a tan could affect my baby, but I was not taking any chances. When you're pregnant, your skin tends to get sensitive, so you need to pay extra attention to your skin.

Seafood

I loved eating fish when I was pregnant. I read somewhere that pregnant women who eat fish would often end up delivering babies with a higher IQ. While that was an added incentive, I just loved eating fish because it tastes great.

Fish has high Omega 3 content. This is important for your baby's brain development. However, the one thing that you should keep in mind is to watch what kind of fish you eat. There are certain fish that have Mercury, and this can be toxic to you as well as the baby. I played it safe and stuck to my favorite fish such as Salmon, canned tuna and catfish. The fish you need to avoid shark, swordfish and king mackerel.

Eat Lots of Fruit

If caffeine was your best friend before your pregnancy, you need to find a new one, and that can be fruits. It is very difficult to give up on the caffeine addiction, but fruits help to lift energy levels, and I found that bananas along with apples were helpful. The natural sugar in fruits are the perfect substitute for caffeine, and they are extremely healthy as well.

Folate-Rich Food

When you are pregnant, you need to make sure you drink a lot of water daily. My magic number was between 8 to 10 glasses daily. Apart from drinking a lot of water, you need to eat at least five well-balanced meals throughout the day. These meals need to be folate-rich such as asparagus, fortified cereals, oranges, wheat germ, lentils, and orange juice. The Folic acid from these foods are critical for the development of the baby, and it is also important in the formation of red blood cells. To sum up, here are a few things I learned from my pregnancy, and I want you to take note.

- Always wear comfortable shoes, so you don't trip or fall
- Wear a seatbelt and sit away from the airbag
- Don't take medication without consulting your doctor
- Stay away from alcohol and smoking. Stay away from people when they smoke

Mindful Pregnancy for New Moms

- Stay away from caffeine products and products that have artificial colors

- Drink plenty of water

- Pee as often as you need to

- Relax your feet to prevent ankle swelling. Sit with your legs raised up as often as possible and soak them in warm water to ease the pain

- Sleep for at least 8 hours and take a nap if you are still tired

Chapter 3:
Morning Sickness No More

Every pregnant woman knows about morning sickness, but they are not sure how to control it or what to expect. Different women react to hormonal changes in their body in different ways. These changes are due to the development of the baby in the womb and it can create a lot of havoc in your body during pregnancy. One of these changes happens to be morning sickness. The term morning sickness itself is misleading because it is usually nausea and vomiting that doesn't necessarily happen in the morning.

While there's little you can do to avoid it completely, I have figured out a few things that can help you understand why you could be suffering from this sickness and what could trigger it so you can try to control it. While almost 70% of women complain of vomiting as well as nausea, there are some women who get through pregnancy without experiencing it at all. From my experience with pregnant women these are the kind of women more likely to suffer from morning sickness:

- A woman is carrying twins or triplets.

- A woman who has a history of morning sickness in the family.

- A woman who has experienced such sickness during their previous pregnancies.

- A woman who usually suffer from motion sickness or migraines.

There are several remedies to treat morning sickness, and you need to figure out which one suits your body best.

Never Stay on An Empty Stomach

Many pregnant women will tell you that when they had an empty stomach, it made their sickness worse. If you do not have an appetite, make sure you eat small meals but eat it regularly throughout the day. This helps lower the chances of morning sickness.

Also, when you continue eating every couple of hours, you make sure your sugar levels and blood pressure stay in control. The best thing to do is keep a lot of bland snacks at hand if you feel the urge to nibble.

Protein-Rich Food

During pregnancy, you should try and eat food that a simple and rich in protein. Protein-rich foods ensure you do not suffer an uneasy feeling in your stomach, and you are able to digest your food properly. You should also eat foods that are rich in vitamin B because this will help keep away the nauseating feeling.

Trying to incorporate as many nuts as possible in your diet and keep away foods that are spicy, rich, fried or acidic in nature. These foods will create an uneasy feeling in your stomach, and you will feel like throwing up more often.

Eat Cold Meals

Don't get excited after reading this! Cold cut meats like Ham or Salami should be avoided during pregnancy because of a possible bacterial infection from these foods.

You need to focus on eating cold meals to take care of your morning sickness. The reason cold meals are preferred over hot meals is that there are women that cannot handle the smell of cooking and they feel nauseated. If cold meals are not helping, then you should consult your doctor, and he will be able to suggest a diet to keep the morning sickness away.

Eat an Early Breakfast

If you have the habit of popping out of bed and rushing to brush your teeth, then you need to stop that habit once you are pregnant. One of the biggest causes of morning sickness is getting out of bed when your stomach is empty. Make a habit of eating a snack in bed and then try getting up very slowly. Something as small as toast can also help prevent morning sickness.

Maintain A Diary

The one thing that helped me get over my sickness was to maintain a diary and note down the peak hours of sickness and the times I felt better. This diary will help the doctor see any trends in your sickness, and he will be able to prescribe medication or even a solution to help get rid of your sickness. Even if you don't want to consult a doctor for your morning sickness, you should go ahead and analyze the diary and see what the best times to eat or drink are. It will also help identify your triggers.

Monitor Your Fluid Intake

While drinking a lot of water is good during pregnancy you should avoid drinking when you are eating a meal. Some women find it very difficult to keep the fluid down, and this can also end up with a vomiting sensation. Do not use this as an excuse for not drinking water when you are not eating. As I said before, drinking about 8 to 10 glasses of water daily is what you should aim at.

Rest A Lot

Every pregnant woman should get at least 8 hours of uninterrupted sleep. Take a quick nap whenever you can because tiredness can often make your sickness worse. However, do not make it a habit to take a lot of naps throughout the day because this will just make you lazy and you will not be able to keep your body active. Too much napping during the day could also be the reason you can't sleep properly at night.

Keep Lemons Around

This may be an old wives' tale, but it works wonders. Smelling a lemon whenever I got a nauseating feeling helped to control it and over a period it helped to prevent the feeling completely. You can also try adding lemon slices to your water or to your iced tea.

Keep Lots of Ginger Handy

Ginger is an amazing ingredient to help your nausea. Adding a little bit of ginger to your morning cup of tea can help settle your stomach. You can also try making ginger syrup or purchasing ginger capsules or tablets from your local pharmacy. You should, however, make sure you consume ginger in moderation as too much of it will result in your throat irritation.

Pregnancy Multivitamins

Although I've said multivitamins help with your health as well as your baby's development, you should know that multivitamins will also control your feelings of nausea. Even if it helps moderately, you should still go ahead and take these multivitamins daily. Irrespective of whether your morning sickness is controlled or not multivitamins should never stop.

Visit A Therapist

There are several therapists who specialize in treating women during their pregnancy. You should go in for aromatherapy or reflexology. These therapies can help you cope and emerge from your sickness.

Sharing Helps

Finally, you could try sharing your feelings with your family members and friends, so they understand what you are going through. Try speaking to somebody who has experienced pregnancy in the past.

She might be able to tell you what remedies you could take or what worked for her. Always make sure you consult your doctor before you begin any kind of medication for your morning sickness. What works for someone else may not necessarily work for you. You need to find a solution that suits your body perfectly, and this can be done when you take the time to understand your body.

Chapter 4:
Nutrition and Food (Must Know Secrets)

Pregnancy is a very important stage in a couple's life because there are more than two lives involved. While it is easy for the partners to see and take care of each other's health, it is very difficult to know what's happening in the womb, and how the baby is coping.

While there are a lot of tests and check UPS that happen on a regular basis to make sure the baby is developing, you need to make sure you take certain precautions and ensure the fetal development is healthy, and there are no hiccups along the way.

There are two components when it comes to making sure you and your baby are healthy. One is the kind of food you eat, and the other is the care you take in terms of vitamins, regular checkups, and tests. Here is my list of the best foods to eat during pregnancy and the best vitamins you can take to help your baby develop in the right manner. You should also check with your doctor with regards to which of these foods and vitamins are perfect for you.

Foods to Eat When You Are Pregnant

Almost every doctor will tell you that you need to eat foods rich in Folic acid, Vitamin D and iron. These three supplements are crucial for your health as well as the development of your baby. The supplements also ensure the cognitive development of the baby happens as per expectations. Everyone wants a baby that's perfectly healthy and intelligent, and these are the foods you should include in your diet to take a step towards a healthy pregnancy.

Green leafy vegetables are healthy irrespective of whether you are pregnant or not. However, the Folic acid in this leafy veggie is important to help with the baby's brain development. Eating the right kind of fruits and vegetables will ensure your baby is protected from any kind of tissue damage. One thing you should remember is to maintain hygiene and wash all fruits and vegetables before you cut into them. This prevents any kind of germ infection, and it will also ensure you and your baby are safe.

When you eat leafy vegetables rich in Folic acid, it reduces any kind of neural tube defects. It also eliminates the risk of a cleft lip as well as all kinds of heart defects that happen in the womb. Eating leafy vegetables also reduces the risk of preeclampsia.

Fish
You may think I love fish because I recommended this before, but certain kinds of fish are highly beneficial for your health and that of your child. Certain fish have high Omega 3 content, and they help with

increasing the baby's intelligence level. Fish such as oysters also help with improving the iodine levels in pregnant women while Salmon helps of the brain development of the baby. You should also be careful about the kind of fish you should avoid, and I will talk about this a little later.

Blueberries

Antioxidants are crucial for health, and this is especially true when it comes to pregnant women. Blueberries are very high in antioxidants, and they help with the cognitive development of the baby. If you live in an area where blueberries are not commonly available, you could always substitute them with raspberries, strawberries, beans, tomatoes or artichokes. This will help with detoxifying your body and making sure that you are clean from within.

Eggs

Eggs are extremely high in protein and very low on calories. Eating one boiled egg daily will help with the brain development as well as memory development of your child. This is because they are known to contain an amino acid known as choline.

Almonds

Almonds are said to be the healthiest nuts available because they are rich in magnesium, healthy fats, vitamin E as well as protein. Almonds are also in Omega 3 which is helpful for your baby's brain development. Eating Almonds daily will reduce the chances of defects in the baby's brain. If Almonds are not easily available, you can also consume walnuts since they are also rich in Omega 3.

Greek

It is important you surround yourself with food that is rich in proteins because this will help to keep the nerve cells healthy of your baby. Nerve damage is something that is often seen in babies, and this can be avoided by consuming food such as Greek yogurt. These probiotic foods are also helpful in the bone development of the baby, and it also helps in preventing low birth weight because it contains iodine.

Cheese

As far as cognitive development of baby goes you need to make sure that you eat foods that are rich in vitamin D. If your Vitamin D intake is low, you will need to get an extra dose of cheese daily to make sure that the IQ level of your baby is high.

Pumpkin Seeds

Zinc is an important mineral that helps with the brain structure formation as well as the cognitive processing of the baby. Pumpkin seeds are not only high in zinc, but they also have antioxidant properties, and they have high nutritional value.

Beans

Iron is essential to help the brain development of your baby. Beans are said to be high in iron, and that's a major reason for you to consume beans regularly. If you dislike beans or they are not easily available, you can pick foods such as figs, spinach, raisins and chicken. If you eat raisins in small quantities daily, it will ensure your sugar levels are in control.

Milk

When it comes to iron, there's nothing better than milk. Milk helps in the development of all the cognitive functions and helps the brain development of the baby.

Vitamins and Nutrients

Your baby gets all the nutrition from you. This means you need to stock up on the nutrient levels in your body for two people rather than just for yourself. You need to keep taking your prenatal vitamins and eat the healthy foods mentioned above. These foods will help you during your pregnancy. You need to make sure you speak to your doctor, and get all the iodine, DHA and Vitamin D medication you need. Never start taking supplements without consulting your doctor.

Prenatal Vitamins

Prenatal vitamins are vitamins meant for pregnant women. They are better than your regular multivitamins, and they have more nutrients that help during pregnancy. You need to ask your doctor for prenatal vitamins when you go in for your prenatal checkup. You need to take the prenatal vitamins daily.

If you are planning to get pregnant, you can start your prenatal vitamins in preparation for your pregnancy. Make sure you check with your doctor before you begin consuming these vitamins.

When pregnant, your body needs all minerals and vitamins in order to stay healthy. Your baby will also rely on you for the nutrient intake. If you are pregnant with more than one baby, you will need to increase your intake of prenatal vitamins. If there are certain foods, you cannot eat or certain vitamins that are not agreeing with you. Speak with your doctor and get an alternative. Ignoring this problem is not the healthiest solution.

Important Nutrients During Pregnancy

There are several important nutrients that play an important role in the development of the baby. They are:

Folic Acid

Folic acid is crucial to the development of the body. If you start taking folic acid before you get pregnant and even during your pregnancy, you will avoid several brain defects as well as spine defects. Folic acid is also known to prevent defects such as a cleft lip or a cleft palate. Your dosage for folic acid should be decided after consultation with your doctor. Ideally, you could start taking folic acid even if you are trying to get pregnant but consuming it during pregnancy, especially during the first 12 weeks, is crucial.

Folic acid is also known to prevent neural tube defects, more commonly known as NTDs. If you have had a high-risk pregnancy in the past, you need to make sure you consume folic acid when you're planning a baby. However, you need to be careful with the number of multivitamins that you consume. Too many nutrients can also prove to be harmful to your health. My doctor helped me figure out the best solution, and you need to do that as well. You need to take folic acid if:

- Your partner already has a child with a neural tube defect (NTD).

- Any of your previous pregnancies had an NTD.

- Either of you has an NTD (you or your partner).

If you do not want to consume too many capsules, you can also eat food that is rich in folic acid. Some amazing foods include:

- Cornmeal

- Breakfast cereal

- Bread

- Pasta

- Flour

- White rice

- Beans
- Lentils
- Leafy greens such as broccoli and spinach
- Orange juice

Iron

Iron is a vital mineral in the body and is used to produce hemoglobin. Hemoglobin is critical in carrying oxygen through your entire body. If you didn't realize it yet, you need twice as much iron when you are pregnant because you are supporting two bodies. The iron from your body will also carry oxygen to your baby's body. The iron is used to create the baby's own blood. Your body needs a certain amount of iron daily when you are pregnant. Your prenatal vitamins will be able to cover the requirement. If you do not want to take any chances you can also include the following foods in your diet that are said to be excellent sources of iron:

- Poultry
- Seafood
- Lean Meat
- Leafy Greens
- Bread

- Cereal
- Raisins
- Nuts
- Beans
- Dry fruits

There are two types of iron your body absorbs. One is heme Iron, and the other is non-heme Iron. You get heme Iron from poultry, meat, and fish. You get non-heme Iron from vegetables, fruits, cereal, nuts, and beans. You receive more non-heme iron when you start eating fruits and vegetables along with your poultry, meat, and fish. You can also include a lot of food that contains vitamin C. These foods include mango, cantaloupe, grapefruit, tomatoes, broccoli, spinach, and cabbage.

If you do not give enough iron, there may be several health complications that may occur. These include:

- Anemia
- Viral infections
- Low birth weight baby
- Premature baby

Calcium

Calcium is an extremely important mineral that aids in the development of your baby's heart, teeth, bones and muscles along with nerve development. While you can get your daily dose of calcium from your prenatal vitamins, you can also consume a lot of food that will provide you with enough calcium. These foods include:

- Kale
- Broccoli
- Yogurt
- Cheese
- Milk
- Orange juice

When you do not receive enough calcium during your pregnancy term, your body takes calcium from your bones and passes it on to your baby. This can lead to severe health complications such as osteoporosis where your bones will become weak and break easily.

Vitamin D

While you need calcium daily, you also need vitamin D to help your body absorb calcium. Vitamin D helps your body's muscles, nerves, and the immune system. It is important for your baby's bones and teeth to grow, and this is where vitamin D comes into the picture. Foods that include Vitamin D are:

- Cereal

- Milk

- Fatty fish

You will also be able to absorb vitamin D when you meet the sun. However, you need to be careful because too much exposure to the sun can also cause harmful effects such as premature aging and cancer. It is best to get your vitamin D from your prenatal vitamins and foods that are mentioned above.

DHA

DHA is docosahexaenoic acid, and it is more commonly known as Omega 3 fatty acid. DHA helps with the development and growth of the baby. It is crucial for the development of the eyes and the brain as well. You should know that not all prenatal vitamins help with providing DHA to your body, so you need to consult your doctor and check if you need to take a DHA supplement apart from your prenatal vitamins. If you do not want to take any additional supplements, you can also consume foods that contain DHA. These include:

- Low mercury fish such as Trout, Salmon, Halibut, and Anchovies.

- Milk

- Orange juice
- Eggs

Iodine

Iodine is another crucial mineral your body needs. Iodine is useful in making thyroid hormones. The thyroid is present in your neck, and it helps to create hormones that assist your body in using and storing energy that it gets from food. Iodine helps the thyroid gland to make hormones and helps your body use energy efficiently. Iodine also helps to develop your baby's brain as well as the nervous system. Iodine is important for your baby's movement, thinking ability and feeling ability. Just like DHA, not all prenatal vitamins contain iodine, and therefore you need to focus on foods that contain Iodine. These include:

- Yogurt
- Milk
- Fish
- Cheese
- Fortified cereal
- Enriched bread
- Iodized salt

What to Avoid Eating and Drinking When Pregnant

I have tried everything that is to know as far as acceptable foods and drinks are concerned, but there are certain foods and beverages you should avoid when you are pregnant. I cannot keep stressing on the fact that you need to stick to a healthy diet when you are pregnant because it helps you stay healthy as well as your child develop properly.

You need to read the package for everything you purchase from your supermarket and pay close attention to everything you eat. There are certain foods you can consume on the odd occasion, while there are other foods that need to stay off the table. These are some important foods and beverages you need to stay away from or try and minimize:

High-Mercury Fish

I know I've spoken about this before, but I cannot stress enough on the fact that mercury is toxic for you as well as your baby. There is no known safe level of Mercury you can consume and therefore its best kept away. Mercury can harm your immune system, your nervous system, and your kidneys.

It is also known to create serious developmental problems to the child in the womb. If you are not sure which fish contain Mercury and which don't, you should know high Mercury fish are only found in polluted seas and are the large marine fish that are high risk. If you feel the urge to eat any of the fish that contain high Mercury, you should consult your doctor before you do. Here are the high Mercury fish you should be aware of:

- Swordfish
- Shark
- Albacore tuna
- King mackerel

Not all the fish that are found in the high seas contain a lot of Mercury. Staying away from fish will keep you away from Omega 3 fatty acids, and this is not good for your health. You need high levels of Omega 3 fatty acids, and you can get this by eating healthy fish. You can always consult your doctor if you are not sure which fish to eat.

Undercooked Fish

There are various varieties of fish that are either served undercooked or raw. Most of these fish are usually shellfish, and they are known to cause various viral as well as bacterial infections. Certain fish also contain parasites, and it is best to stay away from undercooked fish or raw fish as much as possible. Some of the infections from undercooked fish are known to only affect the mother and make her weak and dehydrated. Other infections from undercooked fish can also affect the unborn and can have fatal consequences.

Listeria is one infection that pregnant women need to be careful about. Listeria is a bacterium that is found in contaminated plants as well as water. It can infect raw fish during the processing stage or the smoking and the drying stage. When Listeria is passed to your unborn baby, it can lead to complications such as miscarriage, premature delivery, and stillbirth. This is the reason it is advised that pregnant women avoid raw fish along with shellfish as much as possible. This also includes several Sushi dishes.

Undercooked Meat, Raw Meat, and Processed Meat

Like undercooked fish and raw fish, and undercooked meat and raw meat can also increase your chances of contracting an infection. The bacteria in undercooked meat can affect your unborn and can also lead to several neurological conditions such as blindness, intellectual disabilities, and epilepsy. Most people believe that the bacteria are only found on the surface of the meat. The truth is that there are certain bacteria that are also present inside the muscle fibers. There are certain cuts of meat; however, that can be safe to consume when it is not cooked completely. These include sirloins, tenderloins as well as ribeye. Meat that should never be consumed undercooked or raw includes minced meat, burger patties, poultry, and pork. Certain deli meat, as well as hot dogs, can also contain bacteria, and these are best eaten when cooked properly. If you only have processed meat in the house and you are feeling hungry, you can consume it only after you reheat the meat in hot boiling water.

Raw Eggs

Not many people know this, but raw eggs contain Salmonella. The symptoms of Salmonella are usually experienced only by the pregnant mother and do not pass on to the baby. In very rare cases does the infection pass on to the uterus and when this happens, it could lead to premature birth or stillbirth. There are various foods that also contain raw eggs. These include:

- Poached eggs
- Scrambled eggs
- Homemade mayonnaise
- Hollandaise sauce
- Homemade ice cream
- Certain salad dressings
- Cake icing

In case you are wondering why homemade has been mentioned here, you should know that commercial products contain raw pasteurized eggs, and these are said to be safe to consume. If you crave eggs, you should only consume pasteurized and well-cooked eggs.

Organ Meat

Organ meats are a great source of vitamin A, Vitamin B12, Iron and Copper. All these minerals are great for the mother and her unborn child. However, too much animal-based Vitamin A is not recommended when you are pregnant. It causes something known as vitamin A toxicity, and this can result in liver toxicity and congenital disabilities. While organ meat is recommended for pregnant women, it should not be consumed more than once every couple of weeks. Always consult your doctor for the amount that you should consume depending on your body type.

Caffeine

Caffeine is the most commonly used substance in the world and is found in various soft drinks, tea, coffee, and cocoa. While pregnant women can consume caffeine, they should not consume more than two or three cups of coffee daily. Caffeine is usually absorbed easily, and this passes on to the placenta and the fetus. Since the placenta doesn't have the enzyme to metabolize caffeine, a high level of caffeine will build up and it will restrict fetal growth and cause low birth weight. When low birth weight occurs, there are several complications that could occur such as infant death or type 2 diabetes along with heart diseases.

Raw Sprouts

Like raw meat and raw fish, raw sprouts are also not advisable. Raw sprouts are also known to contain Salmonella. Since raw sprouts require a humid environment to start sprouting, it is perfect for

Salmonella to breed and it is next to impossible to wash off this bacterium. When you are pregnant, it is best to avoid raw sprouts. Sprouts that have been cooked are safe to consume, and you should not stay away from them.

Unwashed Food

Have you ever been in such a hurry that you see an apple in your fruit basket, and you pick it up and start munching on it? You need to avoid doing that when you're pregnant. When you eat fruits or vegetables without peeling or washing them, there are several parasites as well as bacteria that you would be consuming. These parasites and bacteria are usually passed onto the fruits and vegetables through the soil or through the handling of the produce. The bacteria found on unwashed and unpeeled fruits and vegetables are said to be dangerous for the mother as well as the baby. One of the most dangerous parasites called Toxoplasma is found on unwashed fruits and vegetables. Several people get affected by Toxoplasmosis on a regular basis, and most of them feel no symptoms. Most of the infants that are infected with this parasite do not show any symptoms when they are born. However, intellectual disabilities, as well as blindness, may creep in at a later stage in life. A very small percentage of newborns that are infected with Toxoplasma suffer from brain damage at birth.

Unpasteurized Dairy and Fruit Juices

Unpasteurized cheese and raw milk contain a lot of harmful bacteria, and it's the same with unpasteurized juice. All the infections caused by the bacteria found in unpasteurized products can have life-threatening consequences for your baby. Pasteurization is the safest way to kill any kind of bacteria and retain nutritional value. When you are pregnant, it is advisable to only consume pasteurized products especially cheese, milk and fruit juices.

Alcohol

It goes without saying pregnant women should stay away from alcohol completely because it increases the risk of stillbirth and even a miscarriage. While some women feel that a small amount of alcohol on a weekly basis does no harm, they are wrong. The baby's brain development gets impacted by even the smallest amount of alcohol. It is said to cause fetal alcohol syndrome that includes heart defects, facial deformities, and intellectual disabilities. There is no reason to drink alcohol when you are pregnant, and you should avoid it completely.

Processed Junk Food

When you are pregnant, you only need to think about nutrients and calories because it is needed for you and your baby's growth. Your baby needs all the protein, nutrients, iron and folate that it can get. Unlike common thinking, you do not need to eat twice as much because you are eating for two. You just need to eat healthy and eat foods that contain a lot of protein and nutrients. Try to eat whole foods as much as possible because it helps to fulfill the needs of your child as well as your health needs. When you consume processed junk food, you are consuming a lot of sugar, calories and added fat. The nutrient value for junk food is usually very low, and it is best to stay away from this as much as possible. When you consume added sugar that has been added to processed junk food, it increases the risk of several diseases including heart complications as well as type 2 diabetes. It's important to gain weight when you are pregnant; however, excessive weight can lead to various diseases as well as complications. It can increase the risk of gestational diabetes as well as birth complications.

Chapter 5:
Approved Exercises

There is no denying that it is healthy for you to exercise when you are pregnant, but that doesn't mean you should exercise the way you used to, prior to being pregnant. There are a ton of exercises that you should and shouldn't carry out during your pregnancy. You need to figure out which exercises can help you get through these nine months with ease and which ones you should stay away from.

While it is healthy for you to exercise while pregnant, it is also important for you to make sure you consult your doctor to get a go-ahead to exercise.

While most women have a healthy pregnancy and this allows them to stay active for the nine months, there are few situations where certain complications may not allow you to exercise during your pregnancy. You also need to remember that there are different kinds of exercises for each trimester. So, as you grow into your pregnancy, you may need to lower the intensity of the exercise you do and move to calming exercises such as yoga to help prepare your body.

If you have never exercised in your life, and you have been advised to do so during pregnancy, then stick to something basic like walks. However, if you were active and you would like to maintain your fitness levels, then you can opt-in for something more intense, depending on what your body can handle.

Body Changes

When you're pregnant your body is going to go through a lot of changes physically, and therefore you need to accommodate an exercise regime you are comfortable with. Apart from the fact that you will gain weight, it is not recommended for you to run because it could be harmful for your baby. Pregnant women gain a lot of weight around the belly area and the body balance changes making it more difficult to you to stay confident on your feet which is why sudden movements and fast exercises it should be done at a considerably slower pace. Walking is an easy and great way to keep your entire body active during your pregnancy.

When exercising remember not to indulge in any exercise that accelerates your heart rate or exhausts you too much because this isn't good for your child. Any exercise that makes you feel dizzy or lightheaded should also be avoided. If you are wondering what exercises are safe during pregnancy, then below is a list of some exercises most of my friends did during their pregnancy term. I say this again, before you start exercising make sure you speak to your doctor, so you know what you are doing it safely for your baby.

Catherine Emily

Usually, women who have a low-risk pregnancy shouldn't exercise for more than 30 minutes a day for a maximum of 4 days a week. A low-risk pregnancy is a pregnancy that is not constrained by your doctor, and you have no complications.

Every individual is different, and during your pregnancy, you will experience changes that may be unique to your body which is why you need to check your intensity levels and come up with an exercise regime you are comfortable with without stressing your child in any manner. A lot of people wonder what moderate intensity exercises are. This simply defines your level of fitness and how much you can moderately handle. For some women, a 30-minute walk is defined as a moderate exercise while for others it could be much longer.

If you have aches in your joints, do not put too much pressure on them during exercise because this might make it worse. The best way to begin a healthy exercise routine is to always warm up and then cool it down post the exercise. It's difficult for a pregnant woman to be flexible and trust me, even stretching a little would make me feel like a balloon about to pop. So, everything you do needs to be done gently and slowly. Yoga is great, and I did it for a long time during my pregnancy, so I know just how much it helped me relax. However, I stuck to the basic yoga positions that weren't too complicated because I didn't want to attempt something that could result in an injury. The simple stretches can help you through your pregnancy, and apart from keeping your body healthy, it helps your pelvic muscles adjust to the baby growing inside.

Walking

Another way to exercise during pregnancy is walking which is also the safest. Most pregnant women believe that since they are only walking, they need to walk briskly and fast, so they stay healthy and fit. Let me remind you, when you are pregnant, you will not have the best balance. So, whatever you do, do it slowly. Walking briskly not only risks exertion but it also increases the chances of falling. If you think that a 30-minute walk is too little, increase the time that you walk but don't increase your pace. Walking too fast can also cause cramps in your body which will make it extremely uncomfortable to deal with. When you start walking, do it very slowly and gradually increase your pace to something that's not too fast but not too slow either.

Water Sports

Swimming in water is super fun when you're pregnant because it helps to maintain your body temperature and increases your fitness levels. There isn't too much risk of muscle strain when you are in the water. There is no risk of falling and losing balance as well, which is why this is a great pick. Women who suffer from backaches and leg swellings will find water activities highly beneficial. However, some women tend to get a little dizzy in the water, and if that's how you feel, then you may want to stay away from water during pregnancy.

Stationary Cycling

I spoke about cycling and major benefits it has, but it's also risky for women cycle around in a garden because there's a risk of falling. If you want to benefit from cycling during your pregnancy try getting and exercising bike which is comfortable and safe. If you choose cycling you can do it for your first two trimesters only, don't cycle during your third trimester because it puts a lot of pressure on your belly and balancing even on a stationary bike could get difficult.

Weight Training

Lifting weight during pregnancy has no risks as they are not too heavy. However, if you have never lifted weights in your life do not start when you're pregnant, it's not a great time to begin. While weight training benefits the body, it is designed specifically for pregnant women who lead an active lifestyle prior to pregnancy, and if you try doing it only once, you're pregnant, you will suffer from a lot of muscle cramping and pain.

Running

While I am completely against the idea of running during pregnancy because there's always the risk of a fall, if you have been doing this prior to getting pregnant you can continue running through your first trimester as well. However, once your belly grows, stop running because there are balance issues and falling could cause major problems in your pregnancy.

The Kind of Exercises to Avoid

Exercising is extremely safe and is something that every pregnant woman should do. However, there are several exercises that increase the risk of complications as well as injuries. Some exercises can be extremely tiring, and it can cause a lot of discomfort for the mother as well as the child. If you have always loved exercising and you want to continue that trend even when you are pregnant then you need to make a note of the following exercises that need to be avoided:

Heavy Weight Training

Heavy weight training is something that should be avoided when you are pregnant. When you lift heavy weights, it puts a lot of stress on your musculoskeletal system as well as your cardiovascular system.

Breath Holding

There are certain exercises that require you to hold your breath for a certain amount of time. Yoga along with weight training, are classic examples where you need to control the way you breathe, and this is something that can cause a lot of stress. If any of your exercises require you to stop breathing at any point in time, you need to make sure that you stop those exercises immediately.

Lying on Your Back

The first trimester is extremely crucial for pregnant women, and you need to make sure you avoid any kind of exercises that involve lying on your back. When you lie on your back, the blood flow to the fetus gets affected, and this is not good for the health of your baby.

Lying on Your Stomach

Exercises that involve lying on your stomach are not safe irrespective what stage of pregnancy you are in. You need to make sure that you avoid such exercises because it would put a lot of stress on your stomach and your baby. These exercises include abdominal strengthening exercises and Pilates. Although Pilates does not involve you lying on your stomach, it does put stress on your abdomen, and it can cause muscle weakness.

Contact Sports

Intensity sports or contact sports should be avoided when you are pregnant. Sports such a soccer, ice hockey and basketball can cause a lot of stress on your abdomen and can result in abdominal trauma.

Standing Still

There are certain exercises that require you to stand still for long periods. Such exercises should be avoided because it affects the blood pressure and it could put a lot of stress on your baby.

Scuba Diving

Scuba diving is done under very high pressure, and this should be avoided because it has resulted in various congenital disabilities as well as fetal decompression sickness.

Falling

Any sports or exercises that require you to run around with the possibility of falling should be avoided. Sports such as tennis and racquetball are best kept away when you are pregnant.

Altitude Sports

Any sports that are done at high altitudes need to be avoided because this can result in reduced oxygen supply to your baby. Altitude of up to 2500 meters are considered safe however if you experience any kind of altitude sickness, chest pain, shortness of breath or lightheadedness, you need to stop the exercise immediately and consult your doctor.

It goes without saying that you need to consult with your doctor before you begin any kind of physical activity. Being physical is important but putting a strain on you and your baby is not recommended.

Chapter 6:
Money Saving Hacks for Maternity Clothing

Pregnancies are exciting, and most women end up spending a ton of money on maternity clothes they never look back at. Instead of purchasing too many maternity clothes you never use post-delivery here are some interesting hacks I came up with that benefited me through my pregnancy.

Bodysuits

I don't like showing my skin, and I hated it when I was pregnant because my belly kept protruding and pushing my t-shirt a little higher. Bodysuits work wonders because they helped hide my belly and cover it up effectively. It was also comfortable because you don't feel exposed and you can even choose to combine it with a sweater or jacket and add a little style.

If you have a ton of bodysuits in your closet, your pregnancy is the perfect time to make use of them. They stretch perfectly and move according to your body shape making you comfortable in what you wear. Is also a great way to look a little slimmer during your pregnancy?

Bra Extenders

You gaining weight means your bra will get tighter. If you haven't increased in cup size, you don't need to get rid of your old bra and replace it with a new one. I just purchased a few standard bras and was able to wear the existing bras through most of my pregnancy. I decided to invest in nursing bras only after my baby was born only because it was more convenient to breastfeed. Through my pregnancy, I used the same bras that I used prior to getting pregnant.

Using A Hair Tie for Your Jeans

This one may seem a little embarrassing to share, but I am guilty of doing it until my sixth month of pregnancy. I used a hair tie and hooked it inside the slit to accommodate my growing belly to still get the button done. I wore long tops to cover up this hack, but it's kind of benefited me and I didn't have to invest in multiple jeans throughout my pregnancy. It was only during my last trimester that I bought maternity pants. Trust me when I say this, get yourself one black pair of jeans and any other color you think will blend in with your wardrobe perfectly. You don't have to choose expensive branded ones. Even if you get maternity pants at your local store, purchase them because you don't have to deal with them for a long time.

String Bikini

Just because you're pregnant doesn't mean you have to avoid the beach. String bikinis are amazing because you can wear them throughout your pregnancy, and you can just customize the strings as and when you need to. I headed out for a holiday with three pairs a string bikini that I had from my honeymoon. All I did was extend the size of the strings.

Dresses

Maternity dresses gained a lot of popularity back in the 80's. To me, they still look like night dresses that women wear in public. There are dresses that you can purchase and use post pregnancy as well. A t-shirt dress is a classic example of something you can use during your pregnancy and post it. T-shirt dresses look cute, and you can pair them with flat shoes and sneakers to add to your attire. You can also look for stretchable fabric that goes snug around your belly. These dresses can be used post-delivery and still look stylish. Just because you're pregnant doesn't mean you can't look good in what you wear, you just need to make sure you get your hands and clothes that are not labeled as 'maternity clothes.

Sock Boots

Dealing with winters during your pregnancy could get a little difficult if you got a pair of boots that don't fit because of your feet swelling. If you want to invest in shoes, try to get the ones that have a sock built inside of it. This way you can make use of the boots even after your pregnancy because they will never be too big since they are flexible.

Oversized Coats

Jackets and coats look great when they are a size bigger, and when you are pregnant it will fit you just right. This makes it a great choice to invest in during pregnancy.

Quick tip - Don't overindulge in jackets and coats and stick to about one or maximum two that you can use. Pregnant women tend to feel a lot hotter, so you won't be wearing a jacket as much.

Protecting Your Belly Button

There are several expensive clothes that are meant to take care of your sensitive belly button. Rather than spending on such expensive clothes, you can take care of your belly button and make sure that it does not touch any of your fabric. When you reach towards the end of your pregnancy, your belly button will start protruding outward. One of the best things to do is to use a silicone nipple cover and put it on your belly button. This will make sure that your belly button does not rub against your clothing and it does not protrude through your top. There are various silicon options that are available in deep skin tones as well.

Tops That Grow with You

It's hard to believe that there are tops that can grow with you. If you feel that your breasts are growing very large or your stomach is growing rapidly, you can purchase tops that you can tie. This can be done by tying a few of your old scarfs together and making a shirt. This is a perfect kind of clothing to use when it is extremely hot outside, and you will not even have to worry about the shirt not fitting you. All you need to do is tie it around your breasts, and you will be comfortable walking around in the hot sun. Don't forget to apply sunscreen on your belly because this will help protect you and your baby.

Polyester Pajamas

If you have been applying oil or any kind of lotion on your stomach to prevent stretch marks, most of your cotton pajamas will get ruined because they soak up the oil as well as lotions. The best thing to do is to take out your polyester pajamas because they will not soak up anything. All you need to do is wear them when you sleep and wash them when you wake up and it will be as good as new. Using polyester pajamas are a lot more comfortable and an economic option.

Adjustable Bras

If your cup size does not change during your pregnancy, then you can use a bra extender, as I mentioned above. However, if your cup size changes constantly then you will need adjustable bras to keep you comfortable throughout your pregnancy. There are several adjustable bras that are available, and they even come with the nursing option as well as a workout option. You can choose one to depend on what you want to use it for. If you plan on using your bra even after you deliver your baby, then you may want to invest in the adjustable nursing bra.

Don't Invest in Shoes with Laces

For someone that has already gone through a pregnancy, let me tell you that bending over to tie your shoes is extremely difficult and almost next to impossible. It is not even recommended by your doctor, and the only way you can avoid this is by purchasing shoes that you can slip on. Slip-on shoes are available in various colors and various economic options so you can pick one depending on what suits your budget and your preference.

Belly Bands

Belly bands are the latest trend, and several women loves wearing these under a dress or even a loose sweater. This is done in order to avoid any kind of itchiness from the fabric and to keep your dress safe from the oil and creams that you have been applying on your belly. You can create your own belly band at home rather than investing in an expensive one. All you need to do is pull out an old pair of stockings and cut them in half. This half stocking works perfectly as a belly band accessory, and it can be worn under all your clothes.

Kinesiology Tape

The problem with a belly band is it can get curled up and look funny under a dress or a top. You can opt-in for a Kinesiology tape. This tape allows for a seamless look, and it will also support your belly and keep it away from any kind of irritation.

Chapter 7:
First Trimester Essential Secrets

Whether or not you are planning to have a baby, the minute you learn that you are pregnant, it fills your heart with a lot of joy and excitement. There are also several questions that are unanswered, and most women don't know where to start. If you are wondering how you should go through your first trimester, then here are a few secrets you should follow to enjoy your pregnancy to the fullest. Your first trimester is essential because it's the highest risk of your pregnancy and most miscarriages occur during these three months. It takes a while for your baby to latch onto your uterus firmly and that doesn't happen during the first three months. This means you must be careful and make sure you take the pregnancy to full term and avoid any complications.

Arrange an Appointment with Your Midwife
Every pregnant woman makes sure she gets to the doctor as soon as possible. However, what she doesn't remember is it's important for her to schedule a meeting with her midwife as well. Your midwife will spend more time with you during your pregnancy time than your doctor will, so the sooner you get to know here, the better it is. The best

time to get to know your midwife is anywhere between the 10th to the 12th week of your pregnancy. Sometimes doctors choose to introduce the midwife to the pregnant woman even as early as the 8th week. Your first appointment with the midwife will last long because this includes a thorough examination including your lifestyle and your medical history.

Although every midwife will take note of every little detail in your life, you need to have a list ready with you to cross-check just so you are confident she's got everything covered. Some important topics you should remember to cover include

- Your medical history, including any pregnancy complications

- The lifestyle you lead

- All information regarding what you need to do during your pregnancy - including what you should eat and what exercises are safe for your baby

- Make sure to check your blood pressure

- Get your height and weight measured and calculate your body mass index

- Ask for a complete list of all the screening tests you need to go through

Start Your Prenatal Vitamins

If you weren't taking folic acid prior to the pregnancy now is the time for you to start. Once you have spoken about the various vitamins and nutrients, you need to make sure you take a complete list and ask your doctor whether you need to take them and in what dosages.

Ask Before You Take Any Medication

If you are on medication for any sickness or ailment, make sure you ask your doctor whether you can continue taking that medication or whether there is a safer alternative. People who suffer from thyroid and diabetes may need to check with the doctor about the kind of medication they are taking and whether it is safe for the baby or not. Even if you suffer from migraine or certain kind of aches in your body, make sure you ask the doctor what medicines are safe during pregnancy. If possible, get the complete list of safe medications to take and stock up, so you don't end up taking something that's not safe for you.

Quit Smoking If You Are A Smoker

Some pregnant women believe that they can continue smoking until 12 weeks before they quit smoking, but that's far from the truth. If you continue smoking, you are at a higher risk of suffering a miscarriage or any complications within the first trimester. Women that continue smoking during the first trimester are also at risk of premature labor and low birth weight. If your partner smokes, you may have to ask him to either quit smoking or smoke outside the house, so it doesn't affect you or your baby. Remember, second-hand smoke is just as bad as smoking.

Learn About the Danger Signs

It's important for you to educate yourself with regards to the symptoms of pregnancy that are normal and the ones you shouldn't ignore. Slight cramping as your stomach expands is normal, but if your cramps are a little severe like your periods bleeding along with the cramping, you may want to call your midwife or doctor immediately. Don't ignore small symptoms that are not normal, or you think they are going to fade away eventually. The sooner you act upon a signal that indicates danger, the safer you keep your baby.

Rest as Often as Possible

Pregnant women need to sleep a lot, and your first trimester is probably the most difficult time for you because you are not used to resting as much. There are times you wake up in the morning feeling fresh as ever but there will be times you may want to crawl back into bed. This is simply because of the changing hormones in your body and the fact that your body is working harder to keep the life inside you healthy. If you work a regular 9 to 5 job, make sure that you relax as much as possible during the weekends and sleep for as long as you want. If you can practice sleeping on your right side, you may want to try doing it because lying on your back may affect the blood flow to your baby and thus increases the risk of a stillborn.

Prepare to See Your Baby

If your pregnancy is normal and you have no complications, you will most probably be scheduled for an ultrasound between the 10th to the 14th week of your pregnancy. This is the time you will be able to hear your baby's heartbeat for the first time and get an approximate due date. This ultrasound usually takes about 20 minutes, but at times it may take a little longer.

Quick tip - you need to have a full bladder to get a good ultrasound. So, drink plenty of water before you head to the clinic for your scan.

Baby's Development

You need to do anything and everything possible to make sure that your baby is developing properly. While you may take certain precautions and ensure that you are consuming all your vitamins as well as nutrients, you need to follow your baby's development and make sure that the fetus is developing properly, and the heart rate is stable. There are a few apps that are available that will allow you to monitor your baby's development on a weekly basis. Make sure you consult with your doctor before you rely on any of these apps because most of these apps are fake and they may provide false information.

Join A Club

If it is your first pregnancy, there will be a lot of anxiety with regards to what to expect and what not to do. Speaking with other pregnant women may or may not help if they are not delivering in the same month as you. You need to speak with women that are at the same stage as you and would be due in the same month. Join a birth club that segregates mothers based on the delivery date, and this will help you share your experiences as well as learn from the experiences from other pregnant women.

Budgeting

While it is only the first trimester, it is important to budget for the baby and prepare a plan that will help you handle the cost of a growing child. There are a number of expenses that will keep adding up, and you need to make sure that you come up with ideas that will help you save money or look for secondary jobs that can help you increase your income.

Opt-In for A Massage

Pregnancy can be a very stressful period, and you may suffer from back aches as well as headaches. The only way to get through this stressful period is by relaxing yourself and getting a pregnancy massage. You do not need to go to a massage parlor or a spa to get a massage. You can just ask your partner to rub your shoulders along with your back and your head, and this will help relieve any stress or tension you are going through.

Involve Your Partner

Women usually connect with the child from a very early stage in the pregnancy. You will be able to experience all the symptoms and know early on if your child is healthy or not. This connection between a mother and a child is extremely close, and there is nothing that can come between that. But the one person that misses out on all this is the father. Fathers are not able to bond with the baby as much as they would like to because of obvious reasons. Try and get your partner involved in various things such as taking you for your daily walks or helping you plan with the finances or even taking you for your appointments. When the partner gets involved with everything, he will feel a lot better, and he will also try and help to create a better bond with the baby.

Antenatal Classes

When you get pregnant, there are several antenatal classes that you need to look up in your area. These classes get full very quickly, and you need to make sure that you book your classes as early as possible. If you have been planning your pregnancy, it is better to check out antenatal classes even before your pregnancy is confirmed. Most of the classes will enroll you even if you are anticipating your pregnancy in the coming months. It is better to start these classes rather than let your first trimester go by without you knowing how to cope with parenthood as well as labor and childbirth.

Floor Exercises

One of the things that your antenatal classes will teach you is pelvic floor exercises. These exercises will prevent you from leaking while you walk. If you've not been shown how to do the pelvic floor exercises during your antenatal classes, you can always contact your midwife, and she will help you with the same. It is important to continue with pelvic floor exercises during the first semester because this will help your body prepare in the right manner for the rest of your pregnancy.

Household Chores

Household chores are something that cannot be avoided; however, you need to make sure that you stay away from cleaning products as well as chemicals. As stated before, chemicals are very harmful to you and your baby and the fumes that emerge from these can have serious repercussions on your unborn child. One of the things that you should do is keep all your windows open when you are cleaning your house. You should also avoid any products that are available in aerosol cans. If you are a nurse or you work in an area that can expose you to X-rays, then you need to consider changing your job because X-rays are not good for you or your baby.

Exercise

Like I said, exercising in moderation can help you cope with the mental as well as physical demands during your pregnancy. However, you need to be sure that you are as comfortable as possible when you are exercising. While some women try to keep up with their exercising habits even when they are pregnant, you need to make sure that you stay active only by staying within the limits of your comfort.

Announcing Your Pregnancy

Catherine Emily

The first trimester is not only exciting and crucial for the parents, but it is also very exciting for the immediate family members. Some couples do not like to announce their baby until the second trimester because by then the bump becomes very difficult to hide. While it is your choice when to announce your pregnancy, you may want to reveal it during the first semester if you are involved in a job that is dangerous or strenuous. Getting support from family members is extremely crucial during a tough time, and your friends at work can also help you if your job could be potentially dangerous to you or your baby. Talk to your partner and decide when the right time to announce the pregnancy is, depending on the complications with your pregnancy or the complications involving your job.

Chapter 8:
Second Trimester Essential Secrets

Once you're in your second trimester, your baby has secured itself in your womb, and this is around the time you should start getting a little more involved with various activities related to your pregnancy to have a healthy one. Here are a few to do's you should get tick off your list during your second trimester.

Prenatal Exercise Classes
While you should ideally sign up with these classes in your first trimester, if you haven't already done this you may want to do so now. The classes will not only help you stay fit but prepare you for labor. The reason these classes are so beneficial is that you come across other pregnant women and it becomes easier for you to discuss your problems with people who are going to the same bodily changes as you are.

Learn About Your Prenatal Visits
You must visit your midwife at least once a month during your second trimester just to make sure you are healthy, and your blood sugar and pressure is normal. This is also the time you could do a screen

test for down syndrome and other forms or abnormalities in the baby. Genetic disorders and neural tube defects are also usually detected in this trimester. Your ultrasound during the second trimester is something you will thoroughly enjoy because you will be able to see what your baby looks like as he or she takes form.

Make Changes to Your Wardrobe
You don't have to go shopping for maternity clothes and like I discussed in chapter 6, make smart choices and make sure that you have clothes that you are comfortable in.

Decide Whether You Need A Professional Labor Coach
Labor coaches have become popular these days, and a lot of women are hiring them to help with the process of labor and delivery. Labor coaches provide you with a lot of emotional support as well as guidance that helps you get through labor in a more relaxed and comfortable manner. It is always best to have one during the second trimester because you start connecting with them and you manage to discuss the position for delivery you are comfortable with and every little detail about going into labor with ample time in hand. While a lot of people leave having a labor coach for the third trimester, if your baby is premature it will be difficult for your labor coach to assist you because of lack of time.

Plan Adult Time

Once you enter your second trimester your symptoms will probably ease, and you might become more sexually active. It's during these months that you should make the most of your relationship with your partner. Try going out on a date and enjoying being a couple just before the baby arrives so you can feel complete and happy and prepared for the baby even more. It's also important to get intimate with your partner because it helps you feel sexy, and it helps you overcome any doubts you have about your body because of the number of changes that you go through. This is a great time to plan a babymoon because it is safe to travel, and your belly isn't very big, so you'll be able to move around more comfortably.

Start Moisturizing Your Belly

If you want to stay away from stretch marks, you must moisturize your belly as often as possible. As your belly grows, your skin starts to stretch, and it increases the urge to start itching. If you itch your belly, it will get more stretch marks, and it will be difficult for you to get rid of these marks post-delivery.

Narrow Down Baby Names

Most parents always have a list of names that they like but it's not always necessary for partners to agree on the same names. Your second semester is a great time for you to narrow down names by involving the people you want to be a part of the process. The smartest thing to do would be to make a list of the names you and your partner like and share it with the people who you want suggestions from. Select the most popular names and then being narrowing down the list on your own until you are left with a few names that you and your partner are both happy with.

Decide Whether You Want to Know the Sex of Your Baby

During the second trimester, you'll be able to ask your doctor whether you are having a girl or a boy. Knowing the gender is a personal choice. While some parents opt to learn the gender of the baby during delivery, they are others who want to know the sex of a baby before the baby arrives. If you want to have a gender reveal and you do not want to know the sex of the baby before the gender reveal, you can always ask your midwife to hand over the information to the person who is in charge of planning the gender reveal.

Note Down Your Pregnancy Dreams

When you are dreaming, there will be a lot of excitement with regards to the arrival of your baby. These happy thoughts are always healthy for you, and they help you stay in a positive place. It's important for you to note down all these dreams you have so that every time you feel low or unhappy, you can go through the journal and this will lift your spirits almost instantly.

Childbirth Classes

A lot of moms to me wonder why they need to sign up for childbirth class when they are in the second trimester. Believe me when I say this, these classes fill up so fast you may be left with no option but to go into labor without getting involved in the class if you don't sign up during your second trimester. Hospitals offer childbirth classes as well, but you can also choose a specialized childbirth session with your partner. Some parents also choose to have their babies delivered at home and if that is something you are looking to do, educate yourself as much as possible. One-on-one sessions are always recommended because you can have your partner with you and your healthcare provider can give you all the information you need with personal attention to ensure you are covered up.

Financial Planning

There are several responsibilities you must take up when you become a parent, and this includes educational expenses, healthcare, and a good lifestyle which requires savings. Make sure that you plan the expenses for your child in advance so that you can provide a secure environment and give your child a beautiful life.

Prepare Your Pets

It is important for you to keep your pets prepared about your pregnancy and the arrival of your baby because they need to learn and respect and care for the child. Instead of pondering about how you want tu keep your baby away from the pet, try tu create an environment where your pet and your baby get close to each other. You also need to decide for your pet during delivery, so you know someone is caring for your pet when you are in the hospital.

Start Child Care Research

There are various things you need to stay prepared for, and childcare is one of the most essential of them. If you plan on getting back to work after a few months of maternity leave, you need to get the best options for daycare or nanny care depending on what you think will be most feasible for your baby. You could also check and see if it will be possible for you to leave your baby with relatives or parents because this is a safer option.

Teeth Cleaning

That a lot of misconceptions regarding teeth cleaning during pregnancy. Not only is teach cleaning healthy but doing it during pregnancy is also something that is recommended by doctors. When you clean your teeth, you are less likely to transmit cavities and bacteria to your babies. The second trimester is a great time to get your teeth cleaned. When you go for a teeth cleaning session, make sure to inform your dentist about the pregnancy in case it's not obvious.

Celebrate Your Halfway Milestone

It important to celebrate every milestone in your life and 20 weeks is your halfway to pregnancy which is a moment worth celebrating. Indulge in a pedicure or a beautiful massage that soothes your senses. This is a great time to purchase maternity clothes and show off your baby bump with pride.

Sleeping on Your Side

While I already recommended this in the first trimester, you may want to start paying a little more attention to sleeping on your side in your second semester to help with the blood flow to your baby and reduce the swelling. This is where a pregnancy pillow comes in handy because you can slip it between your legs, and it comforts you and helps you sleep better.

Kegels Exercises

While I've done it all my life, you must start doing it during your second semester to help strengthen your muscles and prevent urine leaks which is common during pregnancy. Exercises also help to tone down your vagina, and this has sex more enjoyable for partners.

Baby Registry

Carrying a baby registry is practical, and if you are planning on having a baby shower, this is the first thing you should do. Make a list of everything you need and list it on the registry. While people don't have to buy all of it for you, you have at least half of the list covered up after the baby shower, and this will take off a huge burden from your shoulders. It also ensures that you don't get unnecessary gifts that you will not use.

Talk About Maternity Leave

If you are you working woman and career is important to you, now is the time for you to discuss your maternity leave, keeping in mind circumstances which could include bed rest, premature delivery or complications that could delay or prepone your maternity leave. Try delegating all your work or finishing up as much as possible before you sign off and decide which coworkers will handle your work in your absence.

Check Your Rings and Bracelets

If you wear earrings and bracelets, it is important for you to constantly keep checking if they have become tighter, because your body tends to swell up during pregnancy and if you are wearing jewelry that's too tight it could become uncomfortable. If you don't want to take off your wedding ring, just put it on the chain that will be very close to your heart.

Plan A Baby Shower

While the gift registry is part of a baby shower, it's not all you have to think about. Check for different ideas for the baby shower and let people know what you are looking forward to. While you may not have to plan your own baby shower, you can give people an idea of what you would like for your baby shower, so they know how to plan it.

Avoid Unsafe Activities

If you ride a bike or scooter, you may have to stop during your second trimester because there is a high risk of falling and this could cause trauma to your abdomen. You also need to stop any contact sports or something that involves too many jerks that could affect your baby.

Amusement park rides are also something you must stay away from, and scuba diving is something you must cross off the list.

Write A Letter to Your Baby

It's always beautiful to share your pregnancy experience with your child, and there's nothing better than writing down what your experience is all about as well as your hopes and dreams for your baby while your baby is still in your belly. Make a memento box and keep whatever you think will hold value and will be a cherished memory for your baby when he or she grows up. This memento box could later be gifted to your baby and will be a beautiful procession to have.

Home Improvement

Your second semester is a great time for you to start planning a nursery and space for your baby. If there are any new things you want to bring in, it should be done around this time, and any dangerous or hazardous areas should be fixed almost instantly. You should plan home improvement but try not to be a part of it because exposure to chemicals is not healthy for your baby. As much as you want, you cannot paint because going up a ladder is a complete no-no.

Things to Do During All Your Trimesters (Especially During the Second Trimester)

Pregnancy can be a stressful as well as an enjoyable phase in your life, and you need to make sure that you project the right mindset. The only way you will be able to make sure that you enjoy pregnancy is if you do things right and you keep you and your baby healthy. Here are a few things that you need to do during every trimester to ensure that you and your baby have a wonderful pregnancy.

Drink Lots of Water

Water is essential during your pregnancy, and you need to drink about 8 to 10 classes per day. If you are involved in any kind of physical activity or light training, then you need to add a little extra water to your daily diet. If you think that you are drinking less water than other women, do not worry. Some women need more water than you, and there is a possibility that you may end up drinking more than ten glasses of water daily. The best way to check whether you need water is by checking the color of your urine. If your urine is cloudy or dark yellow in color, then you need to make sure that you drink more water than you currently are. If your urine is pale yellow or clear, then you are drinking the perfect amount of water.

Stretching

While stretching is easier to do in the first trimester, it gets difficult from the second trimester onwards because of the growth of your baby bump. Rather than sitting around and feeling lethargic, you need to make sure that you continue stretching your muscles so that it does not tighten up. When your muscles are losing you will feel a lot more relaxed, and your flexibility will also be enhanced. This proves to be extremely crucial when you go into labor.

Pregnancy Power Naps

While it is important to stay active and keep your muscles loose, you also need to reward yourself with a few power naps through the day. Taking a quick 15-minute nap will make sure that you are energized through the rest of the day and you will be able to get rid of the fatigue that you may be facing. If you are at your workplace, then you can go to the nearest conference room or even close the door to your office and take a quick power nap. Whatever you do, you need to make sure that you have set an alarm on your phone so that you do not oversleep as you may not feel that great after sleeping for long hours in the middle of the day.

Healthy Snacks

One thing that you should be aware of is your hunger pangs will keep getting worse in your second trimester. Since your baby is growing, you will feel a lot hungrier, and you will need to snack every couple of hours. Rather than binge eating unhealthy snacks, you need to make sure that you keep your nutritional snacks ready everywhere you are because hunger can strike anywhere. If your morning sickness has not cleared even during your second trimester, then you can keep your trusted crackers available to eat whenever you feel hungry.

Relax as Much as Possible

Relaxing is very underrated during pregnancy, and you need to make sure that you give your body enough rest and relaxation irrespective of your schedule for the day. Some of the better techniques to employ are prenatal yoga, deep breathing along with progressive muscle relaxation. These exercises will ensure that you sleep better, and you will feel completely relaxed.

Power Walks

I've already touched on the fact that power walks can be dangerous if your belly size is too big. Different women have different belly sizes during the second trimester. If your belly size is not that big and you are comfortable walking, then you can do so provided there is someone along with you. If you are not confident about walking quickly, then you need to avoid it because it could be dangerous for you as well as your baby.

Pregnancy Superfoods

I have already covered all the foods that need to be eaten during your pregnancy. However, your second trimester is extremely crucial, and you need to munch as many superfoods as possible during this phase. Some of the foods include veggies, fruits, yogurt, Salmon, Walnuts, eggs, sweet potatoes and beans. Eating these superfoods at least four or five times a day will make sure that you are extremely healthy, and your baby will grow at a very normal pace.

Start Maintaining A Journal

Pregnancy is an exciting phase in every woman's life, and you may want to share these memories with your child at some point in time. Maintaining a journal and making notes will not any help lift your spirits; it will also make sure that your child appreciates all that you've done to give him or her a healthy life. You will also be able to make sure that you see what triggers your illnesses and what foods you are allergic to. Maintaining a journal during the second trimester is crucial not only from a mental perspective but also from your health perspective.

Weight Gain

By the time you reach your second trimester, you will know what your healthy weight range is and at what pace you are gaining weight. Keeping track of your weight and the progress will ensure that you are taking all the precautionary steps in case something is not right. You should also try not to panic if you do not see too much growth happening in the first couple of weeks of the second trimester. Always stay in touch with your doctor and make sure that he monitors your situation perfectly in order to avoid any unfortunate circumstances.

Do Nice Things

If you are at home and you do not feel too good, there is no harm in heading out to get a pedicure done or to watch a movie. When you do things that you love, you will start enjoying your pregnancy, and this will put you in the perfect frame of mind. Try surprising your partner with a romantic dinner and show him that you appreciate all the support that he is providing you. When you take a break from the stress of pregnancy you will feel relaxed and in a happier state of mind.

Check with Your Friends

That may be times that you come across certain scenarios that you are not sure about and in such situations, it is best to check with a friend that has been through the journey of pregnancy. A friend will be very frank with her experiences, and she will let you know exactly what to expect and what her fears were. While your husband may be away for work for most of the day, you need to make sure that you have someone by your side and a friend can help you in this regard.

Identify Problems

You need to make sure that you identify any problems that you will be facing during your pregnancy and the second trimester is the ideal time to find out these problems and tackle them. Here are a few problems that you need to look out for and contact your doctor immediately:

- If your baby is kicking around lesser than usual or not moving around as much as he or she used to.

- Vaginal spotting or bleeding.

- Vaginal discharge changing from a milky white to bloody or watery.

- After 37 weeks of pregnancy, your mucus discharge should increase. Contact your doctor if this does not happen.

Mindful Pregnancy for New Moms

- Increased pelvic pressure.

- Severe lower back pain (especially if it was not happening during the first trimester).

- Stomach pain or menstrual cramping.

- Experiencing more than six contractions in an hour before your 37 weeks is up.

- Painful burning sensation while urinating.

- During the urge to urinate even after you're gone a couple of minutes back.

- No urination or little urination.

- Blood tinged or cloudy urination.

- Sudden chills or experiencing of your higher than 100.4 degrees Fahrenheit.

- Sudden vomiting accompanied by fever or pain.

- Visual problems such as blurring, double vision, flashing lights, dimming or spots in your line of vision. These are all probable symptoms of preeclampsia.

- Puffiness around your eyes or swelling in your face.

- More than normal weight gain.

- Any kind of abdominal injury due to a fall or a minor accident.

- Persistent itching of your arms, torso, legs, soles or palms.

- Pain in your shoulder or upper belly.

- Flu-like symptoms such as cough, sore throat, sudden fever, stuffy or runny nose, body aches, exertion or sudden chills.

- Frequent vomiting or diarrhea.

- Profound feelings of sadness or hopelessness can lead to panic attacks or depression or even anxiety.

- Any of your current health problems getting worse such as worsening asthma.

Take Photos of Your Belly

Parents love documenting the progress during pregnancy and taking photos of your belly is a great way to do that. Not only will you be able to monitor the progress, but you will also be able to collect a lot of memories and share them with your child at some point in their life.

Chapter 9:
Third Trimester Essential Secrets

The third trimester is the final stage before your baby arrives. This trimester should be focused completely upon preparing for the arrival of your baby and making sure you are as prepared as you can be to go into labor. Here is what you need to do to prepare effectively for your third trimester.

Beware of Your Baby's Movements

Your baby is going to move around in your belly a lot during the third trimester, and you will figure out a pattern in the movement of your child within a few weeks. Your baby will also sleep, so you will figure out when your baby is resting and when your baby is awake. You will also realize when your baby is moving towards labor, and this is the time you need to contact your midwife or doctor immediately.

Learn About Third Trimester Antenatal Appointments

This is the final step of appointments you must go thruugh prior to going into labor, and this always includes preparation for labor and birth as well as understanding how you can recognize the signs of labor and deal with labor pains when they happen. This is around the time you will realize how big your bump has grown and you can check your baby's growth depending on the measurements. You can also go for an ultrasound during your third trimester, and this is going to give you a full view of your baby.

Most first-time mums need to go through something that is known as a membrane sweep during the 40th week. This usually helps induce labor, and in case it doesn't, you must go through another one during your 41st week. Women who are having a baby for the second time usually go through this sweep in the 41st week.

Be Cautious About Pregnancy Signs You Shouldn't Ignore

Your third trimester is probably one of those times where you believe you are going to face a lot of pains and cramping which is why you try to look for some warning signs. If you know that your baby isn't moving as much, it's important for you to call the doctor immediately and let them know that something isn't right. While your midwife will ensure that she gets everything covered for you in all the tests to keep your pregnancy healthy, you need to always look out for signs such as you are feeling your blood pressure is a little high or you are suffering from a severe headache or blurred vision. Nausea and vomiting are also signing you shouldn't ignore during the third trimester.

Eat Well

This is something you must do throughout your pregnancy, and I say it again, during the third trimester you must stay healthy and include as much iron rich food as possible to help form the red blood cells in your baby. A lot of lean meats and green leafy vegetables are highly recommended, and you can always wash it down with a big glass of orange juice to help your body absorb the iron more effectively.

Start Stretching

You need to loosen up your body for birth, so stretching is recommended because it helps to release the body from the pain of contractions and prevents cramping, especially in the legs during the time of labor. Just move around slowly and stretch gently to keep your muscles relaxed and ensure that there is no cramping.

Massage Your Bump

Massaging your bump has plenty of benefits. It helps you connect with your baby, and it also increases closeness when you feel your little baby kick. Encourage your partner to rub your belly with gentle strokes to increase the connection and always wait to do this when you know your baby is going to be most active. When you feel your baby kick inside of you, it brings you a lot of joy, and it makes the entire experience worthwhile.

Put Together Furniture and Buy A Stroller

When you have the nursery or your baby space set up, make sure to purchase the right furniture for your baby. Don't spend on too many items because these aren't going to be used forever. You should instead focus on the ones that are essential. A bassinet and a stroller are highly recommended because you will need both items for a while after the baby arrives, and it will make life easier. The reason it is good to put up the bassinet and purchase a stroller now is that you will not need to stress about it once the baby arrives.

Talk to Your Baby

Even your partner should spend a lot of time talking to your baby because your baby can hear voices and start recognizing them from the womb itself. Listening to soothing music and reading a book or a magazine to your baby is something that will make your baby feel connected with you. You can also sing to your baby and make your baby feel happy. It is also important for you to stay calm and composed during the last trimester because the more you stress, the more your baby senses it, and it increases insecurity. Create a happy atmosphere around you if you want your baby to be healthy.

Identify the Signs Of labor As Well As the Stages

It's not easy to predict when labor will strike or how long it is going to last but understanding the procedure can help you control the situation and feel more relaxed. There is a total of three stages of labor which include the contractions, the actual delivery, and the placenta. Make sure to cover up all these three stages, so you have information about what lies ahead and how you must deal with it.

Birth Plan

The third trimester is the perfect time for you to discuss the birth plan and see how you want your baby to be delivered. Whether are you looking for a vaginal delivery or a C-section, it's always better to be prepared for both because sometimes women who want to go for a vaginal delivery may not be able to because of certain complications and they may have to head in for a C-section. Being prepared for both kinds of labor just helps you relax during the process irrespective.

Contraction

The first time that you start getting labor contractions, it is going to begin very gently and eventually escalate into the real labor pain. It begins with the muscles in your worm starting to tighten from time to time. Almost all women go through this pain while some may just go into labor without any contractions whatsoever. The interval between each contraction is what determines how soon you are going to deliver so it is important for you to keep track. Contractions usually occur at regular intervals, so it is important for you to notice how far apart they are because this will determine how long it is before you get into labor. It's important for you to also learn how to deal with contractions because stressing during this time could make it more difficult for you to deliver a baby. The best way to deal with contractions is to have your partner by your side and guide you through the process. You can try practicing this in advance so that you do not have to stress when it happens.

Buy Clothes for The Baby

If you haven't gotten all the essentials that you need for your baby through the gift registry, make sure to purchase everything else that's needed well in advance. If you were given these clothes as a gift during your baby shower, you need to make sure that you wash them with non-biological washing powder and keep them ready for your baby to wear.

Pack Your Hospital Bag

It's important for you to make sure you get your hospital bag ready and add everything inside it so that you don't stress out during your stay at the hospital. I will discuss all the essential items you need to pack in your hospital bag in Chapter 11 so you can take notes.

Sleep

I can't stress on this enough but trust me when I say sleep! These are the last few months that you can relax before you go into labor and then there are going to be a few months of sleepless nights. So, you need to rest as much as possible during pregnancy so that you have the energy to look after your baby. When you sleep, it helps to relax your body, and it also keeps your baby calm. It's important for you to sleep on your side because this reduces the risk of stillbirth and it helps your baby's blood flow to be constant.

Household Supplies

Your baby is approaching soon, and you will need to make sure that you make your life a lot easier right now because there could be a lot of your time taken up with the baby. You need to start stocking up on your household supplies and purchase things that your family may need when you are not able to take care of them post-delivery. These include tinned foods, cleaning products or even frozen vegetables. The reason you need to do this is because shopping will become a huge task and you need to give all the attention to your baby when he or she does arrive. You should also try and cook up a few portions that you can freeze ahead of your first few weeks of being a new parent. This will take away the stress of having to cook while your baby is in your arms.

Baby Car Seat

Most women have a baby in a hospital and going home by car can be quite difficult for the baby as well as the mother. You need to make sure that you keep the baby as comfortable as possible and installing a baby car seat will help you as well as your baby sit comfortably while going back home. You get various car seats depending on your baby's weight. You need to pick the right one and get it installed by professionals so that it is fitted properly. Never buy one because it looks good. It needs to fit your car perfectly, and the belt should fasten without too much problem.

Third Trimester Sex

If your pregnancy is not filled with complications and you and your baby are healthy, you can continue having sex right until you go into labor. You will need to speak with your doctor with regards to the positions that you can have sex in because the pump will keep getting bigger as the days go by. You need to think of your comfort level along with your baby's comfort level.

Get as Much Help as Possible

Do not be afraid to ask for favors because friends and family members will always be there to help. Feeling guilty is not going to help you because your friends and family members are just waiting for you to ask and they will be ready to help in any way possible. Make the most of these helpers and get them to tidy up the house or even help when the baby comes back home. It is always better to have women around that have undergone pregnancy as they will be able to give you better advice and take care of you in a much better manner.

Check the Hospital

If you have decided to have a baby in a hospital, then you need to make sure that you take a tour of the hospital. You can also check the route that you will take to get to the hospital so that you do not get stuck in traffic. You also need to make sure that you check the hospital's policies with regards to insurance and book your room as soon as possible so that you are staying in comfort.

Keep Your Back Healthy

Your back is very crucial during the third trimester as you head into labor. You need to keep it as healthy as possible, and if your bump is giving you any kind of aches in your back, then you need to make sure that you try to avoid any heavy lifting or putting any strain on your back. If the pain is too much, you can even speak to your physiotherapist and get a maternity belt that will help support your back.

Prepare Well

You need to make sure that you and your partner are synced with regards to the childbirth and you have everything in order. You need to have your midwife's number as well as your doctor's number available. If you have other children or pets, then you need to arrange for someone to come and take care of them when you and your partner move to the hospital for delivery. If your children or your pets are alone at home while you are in delivery, it may put additional stress on you, and this is not good for you or the baby.

Hypnobirthing

Hypnobirthing is the latest trend that is catching up these days, and you can speak to your doctor regarding the hypnobirthing techniques. These are nothing but visualization as well as breathing techniques that will help you stay extremely calm and in complete control when you are giving birth.

Read as Much as Possible

If you been reading about pregnancy for the first two trimesters, then you need to start reading about babies in the third trimester. You need to read as much as possible regarding baby care because you will not have time to read once your baby is here. You need to see how the first few weeks will change your life and what you can do to ease your stress.

Breastfeeding

You need to start preparing for breastfeeding and understand how it works as well as realize its benefits. While breastfeeding is natural for some women, it can get complicated for others, and you need to make sure that you are successful at it. You may want to attend a breastfeeding class when you are pregnant, and this will help you prepare in the right manner.

Natural labor

These days it is very common for doctors to induce labor because they are not sure what causes natural labor to start. If you feel that you are overdue, and you are not going into labor, you may want to try some of the various things that can bring about natural labor. These include having sex, walking, eating curry or even acupuncture.

Baby Development

The third trimester is extremely crucial for your baby, and you need to make sure that you follow your baby's development as closely as possible. Tracking the development on a weekly basis will help you feel relaxed and take preventive measures whenever necessary. The closer you get to your delivery, the better it is that you stay prepared for any complications. Tracking your baby's development is the best way to stay in control of your pregnancy and taking care of your child in the right manner.

Chapter 10:
Prevent Stretch Marks Hacks

Stretch marks are common, and 90% of women get them during the sixth or the seventh month of pregnancy. Stretch marks make your skin look bad, and women try to do whatever it is in their power to keep them away. While there is no proven method for you to keep stretch marks away or avoid them completely, there are a few hacks that you could try to reduce the marks, depending on your skin type. I know several women who have gone through pregnancy, but some of them have stretch marks on the stomach while others have a stomach that is smooth. While I did care if there were stretch marks on my stomach, they weren't as bad as some of my friends. It is healthy to accept your scars because it reminds you of what you've been through. This doesn't mean you can't try to keep them away. Here are a few things about stretch marks that I figured out based on my friends and their pregnancy.

- Stretch marks are genetic. A lot of my friends had mothers that complained about them having similar marks on their belly.

- Women who gain more weight during pregnancy get more stretch marks.

- Dark skinned moms are less likely to get stretch marks in comparison to the others.

Stretch marks are basically tiny tears that occur in the layer of tissue under your skin because it's pulled to its limit during pregnancy. While it can't be avoided completely here is what you can do to try and reduce the risk of stretch marks during pregnancy.

Eating Right
It's necessary for you to eat right during pregnancy. Apart from help with the development of your baby, a lot of people don't know that the right food can also help control stretch marks on your stomach. This is because when you have enough vitamins and nutrients in your body, it benefits your skin and enhances the elasticity which limits the risk of a stretch mark from occurring. Foods that are rich in antioxidants can help keep your skin strong and flexible. Include berries and a lot of spinach in your diet if you want to limit the risk of stretch marks. Vitamin E protects the membranes of your skin cells which limit stretch marks, and therefore you need to consume a lot of avocados and greens. Vitamin A helps with skin tissue repair so vegetables like carrot, sweet potatoes, bell peppers, and squash work wonders. Omega 3 keeps cell membranes healthy and helps your skin get a

beautiful glow as well as moisturizers it. Foods like fish and fish oil are great.

Exercising

Exercising helps to retain the elasticity of your skin, and this also enhances circulation which makes sure you don't put on too much weight. It's the weight gain at an accelerated rate that is one of the leading causes of stretch marks, and when you gain healthy weight during your pregnancy, you automatically limit the risk of getting stretch marks.

Watch Your Weight

Women believe they need to put on a lot of weight during pregnancy and this is a big misconception. While you do need to have a certain amount of weight gain to have a healthy pregnancy you don't have to gain so much weight that you end up being obese because this will simply increase stretch marks, and it will make you unhealthy. The key to staying healthy during your pregnancy is to eat smaller meals at regular intervals and eat healthy food rather than unhealthily, and weight gaining food items.

Staying Hydrated

Drinking lots of water does not only take care of your health as well as your baby's health, but it also provides several other benefits. Water is a great source of detoxification and it also helps your skin cope with all the stretching. When you drink a gallon of water daily, you will improve the elasticity of your skin and all the toxins from your body will be eliminated. You should also try and include food that has a high-water content as this will help you stay hydrated throughout the day. When your skin stays hydrated, there will be no stretch marks that will appear because the hydration helps the elasticity of the skin. Including foods such as strawberries, watermelons and cucumbers will help your skin stretch very easily and will keep stretch marks away.

Avoid Chemicals

There are several body washes that are said to contain harsh chemicals. These chemicals not only dry your skin, but it will also affect the elasticity of the skin over a period. You need to start looking for body washes and cleansers that are made using natural oils. These natural oils will help hydrate your skin, and it will make it a lot more elastic. If you are not sure which cleanser you should purchase, then you can also use coconut oil as a skin cleanser. All you need to do is rub it all over your skin and then rinse the oil off with warm water. When you do this, you need to pat yourself dry using a soft towel, and your skin will feel refreshed in no time.

Using Supplements

A lot of people lose the elasticity of their skin as they grow older, and once this happens to your skin, it can never return to the size that it was. Often it is the diet that you eat that also contributes towards your skin losing its elasticity. If your diet does not give you proper nutrients as well as vitamins, then you need to take a few supplements that will help improve the elasticity of your skin. Some of the supplements that you should opt-in for are:

- Vitamin C supplements that are essential for producing elastin as well as collagen.

- Vitamin E supplements that will purify your skin and work as an antioxidant.

- Vitamin D supplements that help with the creation of new growth cells in the body.

Massage Your Tummy

You no longer need to purchase any expensive creams that promise to keep away stretch marks. These creams do not achieve anything, and they are not going to keep stretch marks away that easily. One of the benefits of investing in these creams is it helps to moisturize your belly and it will keep away the dryness as well as itchy skin. When you are pregnant you will need to take care of stretch marks around your tummy, your lower back, your legs as well as your thighs. These are the parts of your body that undergo a lot of strain when your baby is growing inside you. The skin around these areas will keep on itching; however, you need to make sure that you keep the skin moisturized in order to prevent any marks from forming.

Mindful Pregnancy for New Moms

Avoid investing in ordinary moisturizers because they will not be able to penetrate the skin properly. You need to make sure that you invest in a lotion that will help penetrate your skin and prevent any marks from forming. You need to apply this lotion on your most prone areas at least twice a day. Some of the lotions that you invest in should contain collagen, cocoa butter, shea butter, and elastin. These elements help the elasticity of the skin. You can also look for a firming butter that has Vitamin E as well as ginseng in it. These elements help to rejuvenate the skin and soften it. Whichever lotion you invest in, you need to make sure that you massage your belly properly after applying it because this will help the lotion penetrate and give relief and keep away the stretch marks.

Chapter 11:
Necessity Bag Items to Bring for Labor

Going into labor is quite stressful and heading to the hospital is the first thing that comes to your mind the minute you hear the word contractions. There is a reason why I mentioned you should keep your hospital bag ready to just pick up and leave when you head out to the hospital but what you need to put inside the bag is also crucial. The sooner you start packing your bag, the less likely it is that you will miss out on anything. The best way to ensure you have everything covered is to make a list and take off everything that is added to the bag. Here is a list that I prepared for myself and found extremely helpful.

Hospital Id and Paperwork

You need to make sure you carry the hospital identification proof that is needed as well as any other documentation including insurance, if you have it covered for your maternity. Try making a few copies and create a file that you slip into your hospital bag. Make sure you neatly arrange all the documents and keep copies available to pull out easily when needed. Ask the hospital are the documents you and your partner need to carry and keep those ready in the bag as well.

Birth Plan

If you have a good plan ready, make sure to print it out on a paper and get a few copies of it handed out to the doctors in case that is something you want them to understand in specific, and you are in too much pain to discuss. Inform your partner about this copy and make sure that your partner keeps them ready when the time arrives.

Bathrobe

It's important for you to have a soft bathrobe ready with you because this is the most comfortable attire you can wear when you are in labor. It's also convenient to slip back into the robe post-delivery when you are recovering. Some hospitals allow you to wear whatever you are comfortable in during delivery and I chose to wear a bathrobe because it was so convenient and comfortable.

Socks

The labor room usually has the AC at a very low temperature so you may tend to get cold feet - literally! A good pair of socks can keep your feet warm during labor.

Slippers or Flip Flops

You will need a nice comfortable pair of slippers or flip flops that you will need to wear when you walk around the hospital for the delivery as well as afterward. Do not opt-in for shoes that you need to struggle to get into or something that requires bending because this will be too much of a hassle.

Lip Balm

Your lips will dry out when you visit the hospital, especially during labor so keeping a lip balm by your side can help you feel comfortable and hydrate your lips.

Body Lotion or Massage Oil

When you are stressed the best thing to do is get yourself a massage or ask your partner to do it for you, and in this situation, body lotion and massage oil can come in handy.

Water Spray or Sponge

If you start feeling hot during labor using a water spray around your face and neck or keeping a sponge on your forehead can help cool you down. Inform your partner with regards to what needs to be done in this situation and how to keep the water spray or sponge ready.

Entertainment

For some people labors are quick, but for others, it could go on for days so always prepare yourself for the worst and go prepared. You will most likely spend a few hours before you are in labor and the best way to keep calm is to entertain yourself by reading a book or a magazine on even listening to some soothing music.

Eye Mask and Ear Plugs

It is good to keep an eye mask and ear plugs ready when you require to rest. This will keep away any interruptions.

Night Gowns

While the bathrobe can help you during labor, you need something to stay comfortable for the days that you may spend in the hospital and a loose nightgown is the perfect choice. You may want to shop for a night gown and choose a front opening one that can make it convenient for you to breastfeed.

Maternity Pads

Your hospital will provide you with these, but it is always necessary to pack an extra box just in case. Maternity pads are bigger and softer in comparison to normal sanitary napkins. They are used after your delivery or even at times when you need something that is super absorbent. You will need to wear one post-delivery and you may have to change your pad every one or two hours post-delivery so purchasing your own box of Maternity pads will help you through these hours.

Underwear

Make sure that you pack many pairs of comfortable and large underwear that can accommodate the heavy-duty maternity pads you need to use for a few days.

Bras

Get your hands-on nursing bras that are made of cotton and will not hurt you. I had spoken about this in chapter 1, and I repeat this again, always look for cotton and soft nursing bras because when you start breastfeeding, it could be a little uncomfortable, and your body will take a while to adjust to lactation and breastfeeding.

Toiletries

Pack a lot of tissues, your hairbrush, your comb, your deodorant, toothpaste and toothbrush, shampoo, hair conditioner, hair clips, and hair ties and spare plastic bags to keep dirty clothes in.

Cosmetics

If you like wearing makeup on a regular basis carry just the basic like your lip liner, lipstick, eyeliner, and moisturizer. Don't forget sunscreen for when you leave the hospital.

Glasses or Contact Lenses

If you are carrying magazines and books to read, you will need your glasses so don't forget to pack them.

Phone and Charger

It's really important for you to stay in touch with your loved ones when you are in the hospital and the best way to do it is with your phone so make sure to pack your charger and your phone, so you can use it.

Clothes

You need a clean pair of complete clothes to wear when you leave the hospital so pack something that you know is easy to slip on and will keep you comfortable on your journey home.

Snacks and Drinks

Labor could be long sometimes, and if you feel hungry in between, you can always have a quick snack or a drink to sip on. Remember to pack your favorite snacks because you may start craving for this once you've delivered.

Packing Hospital Bag for Your Partner

Your partner is also extremely crucial to the process of delivery, and he will also need a hospital bag to help him function in a better manner. Here are a few hospital bag essentials for your partner.

Snacks Along with Water

Labor can be a very stressful situation for you as well as your partner. You should always consider packing in a few snacks along with a couple of water bottles for your partner in his hospital bag. Also, make sure that you pack as much change as possible for the hospital vending machine.

Gadgets and Chargers

Gadgets such as cell phones, cameras, and video cameras are essential when you are capturing something as beautiful as childbirth. Your partner will need a phone to stay in touch with the other family members and friends that could not make it to the hospital. He will also need the camera as well as a video camera to capture all the memories and click some happy pictures once the baby has arrived. These pictures are memories for a lifetime, and this is something that your partner needs to do in order to look back fondly on these memories later.

Clothes
Your partner should always carry an extra set of clothes because labor could be ongoing for long hours, and in some cases even days. You need to make sure that he is always comfortable, and this is where a change of clothes will come in handy.

Toiletries
Toiletries are essential for your partner when you are in labor or post-delivery as well. Most hospitals allow the partner to freshen up in the hospital shower and if that is the case, you may want your partner to carry along his body wash as well as a personal towel.

Spare Lenses
If your partner wears, contact lenses then you may want to make sure that he carries an extra pair as this could come in handy. As I said, it can be a long day in labor, and this could put a lot of stress on your partner.

Inflatable Pillow
Asking your partner to pack his own pillow may not be very feasible, and this is where an inflatable pillow can come in handy. This will allow your partner to catch a few winks every now and then if the labor process is getting too stressful.

Entertainment Options

Carrying a few things to stay entertained can be useful. Some of these things should be a tablet or even the latest book or maybe a music player that you can plug in and listen to your favorite songs. You and your partner need to do everything possible in order to relieve the stress and entertainment is the best way to take your mind off all the physical and mental strain that you will be going through.

Packing Hospital Bag for Your Baby

While you may pack a hospital bag for you and your partner you should not forget the needs of your baby. Your baby will need a few things when he or she arrives and keeping a hospital bag ready for your baby is an extremely smart thing to do. Here are a few essentials in your baby's hospital bag that you should not forget about:

Bodysuits

Most hospitals will usually provide your baby with a few clothes to wear. Some hospitals would even have policies with regards to what the baby can and cannot wear post birth. You may want to check with the hospital and carry a few extra layers of clothing in case you feel that the temperature is too cold. Always opt-in for bodysuits that can be fastened upfront so that it will be comfortable to put on for the baby and you will not have to worry about hurting the baby as well.

Booties and Socks

It is essential to keep your newborn baby warm all the time, and this is where booties and socks come in handy. You may also want to carry a hat for your baby if you feel that the lighting in the hospital room is too bright. This will also help for the first few weeks after birth.

Homecoming Outfit

Your baby coming home for the first time is a very important milestone, and you need to make sure that the baby is very comfortable and looks good at the same time. You also need to consider weather conditions and see what will suit your baby the best. If the weather outside is warm, you can consider dressing the baby in a bodysuit along with hat and booties. If the weather is too cold, then you will want to carry a jacket or a snowsuit along with mittens for your baby. You need to remember that your baby will not be able to tell you if he or she is comfortable or not. You need to recognize the baby's condition and make sure that you are making the right decision on their behalf.

Blankets

Most hospitals will usually provide plenty of blankets in order to keep the mother and the baby warm post birth. However, carrying your own blanket is essential because this will be helpful when you are taking your baby back in the car where you will need to wrap up the baby. A blanket is also helpful when relatives and friends come to visit the baby, and they may want to carry the baby. A blanket is a great way to avoid skin to skin contact with other people because the baby may not like everyone's touch. Here are a few more essentials that you need to do when you arrive with your partner at the hospital.

Speak to The Staff

When you arrive at the hospital, you need to make sure that you speak with the hospital staff and make the ambiance as amiable as possible. You can ask the staff to lower the lighting or even have special food arrangements done if you are allergic to something. While it is advisable to carry your own food, there is always the possibility of you running out of food, and this is where you need to make the hospital staff aware of your allergies and your diet.

Accommodations

You also need to look at hospital accommodations and make sure that you have a private room along with a private bathroom. You also need to make sure that your room is big enough to accommodate your partner for the night and there is enough room for you to walk around while you are preparing for labor.

Chapter 12:
Essential Recovery Secrets After Birth

Childbirth is not easy irrespective of what method of delivery you have chosen. Once your baby enters the world, it's a lot of excitement and happiness, but it's also the period of your recovery. Once your baby is into the world, you now need to give your body enough time to relax because it needs to adjust to the various changes.

There is no fixed time for how long your body is going to take to recover because different women required a different amount of time to heal depending on the postpartum symptoms. Most of your problems ease away within a week, but others may take a longer time to heal. Sore nipples and backaches are common symptoms that may last longer.

Vaginal birth may seem like it is the easier route for most women, but you still need to rest your body in order to recover completely. Your perineum will take a few weeks to heal depending on if you had a perineal tear or an episiotomy. An episiotomy cut is one of the most painful cuts that you can experience but thankfully not a lot of women go through this nowadays. Always try to avoid the episiotomy cut as much as possible and don't use it unless necessary. This is usually a cut made from the perineal area right up to the rectum to make way for the baby's head to come out during a vaginal birth. A vaginal tear, on the other hand, is a tear that happens naturally when a woman's vagina starts to stretch for delivery. There are different kinds of vaginal tears and while the first degree of a vagina tear is only the first layer of skin, the second degree could include muscle rupturing as well which will take a longer time to heal.

A C-section will require even longer, and if you've been through a c-section, then you may want to consider spending an extra few days in the hospital to enhance the healing process. For your body to completely recover from a C-section, you need to rest a lot, but sometimes it could take a little longer. What's important is that you give your body enough time to heal and ensure that you do not stress too much post-delivery so that you recover completely.

Bleeding After Birth

Postpartum bleeding, which is also known as lochia, usually lasts about six weeks after delivery. It will be like a heavy period that takes out the leftover blood from your uterus along with all the other waste material that your body needs to discard. The first three to 10 days are usually very heavy, and this blood is the extra blood that is getting out of your system which will also include blood clots. You will need to change your pad once every 1 to 2 hours. You must rely on heavy-duty maternity pads which is why I highly suggest you carry a couple of them on your way to the hospital. Women that are used to tampons need to stay off them during the healing process because you will be too sensitive to insert a tampon.

Postpartum Depression

Most women believe that they will not suffer from postpartum depression because of the excitement and joy of having a baby, the truth is postpartum depression happens for most women, and they tend to feel hopeless, isolated, irritable, anxious and sad during this time. With all the attention on your baby, you are bound to feel left out, and this will increase the depression. Postpartum depression affects about one in three new moms, and you need to understand that the sooner you accept you are feeling depressed, the sooner you will be able to get help. You need to recover quickly because this will not only affect your baby, but it will also affect your own health. Postpartum depression could be overwhelming but when you don't deal with it effectively not only will you overcome it, but you will actually start enjoying the true meaning of motherhood, and you will manage to accept the changes that have occurred in your life.

Postpartum Healing

Healing postpartum is essential, and there are several steps that you need to keep in mind to make the healing process faster. Keep the steps in mind to make your postpartum healing a lot quicker.

Perineum Healing

You need to make sure that you give your perineum enough time to recover and you need to apply ice every couple of hours once you have given birth. You need to also make sure that you spray enough warm water over the area before you urinate and even after. This will make sure that the urine does not irritate the torn skin. You can also try taking warm baths for about 20 minutes more than a couple of times a day. This will help to ease the pain and accelerate the recovery process. You should also make sure that you do not sit or stand for long hours. Even when you are sleeping, you need to sleep on your side.

C-Section Scar

If you have had a C-section, then you need to make sure that you clean the c-section area gently at least once a day with soap and warm water. You need to then try the area with a clean towel and apply some sort of antibiotic ointment that your doctor may have suggested. You should also speak to your doctor if you need to leave the wound open or cover it up. Apart from carrying your baby, you should avoid carrying anything else and stay away from vigorous exercise until your doctor gives you the go ahead.

Try to Ease Your Aches and Pains

Once you have delivered your baby, there will be a lot of aching because of the amount of pushing that you have been doing. You can speak to your doctor to provide you with a painkiller or some sort of sedative that can help you forget the pain that you are going through.

You could also opt -in for a hot shower or use a heating pad that can help comfort the area where you are sore. Getting a light massage from your partner can also help take care of your aches and pains.

Regular Bowel Movement

The first bowel movement that you have post-delivery will take a lot of time, but you do not have to push it. You should consume a lot of food that is rich in fiber and try and go for walks daily. If all of this is still not helping, you can even use a gentle stool softener that will help you become regular. You should not push too much because your C-section scar may tear.

Kegels Exercises

In order to relieve your vagina from all the stress and bring it back in shape, you need to make sure that you do your Kegels regularly. You should make sure that you start your Kegels exercises as soon as you are comfortable and do three sets daily.

Aching Breasts

It is normal that your breasts will start aching once you have delivered because the process of breastfeeding must begin. In order to treat your sore breasts, you can start using ice packs or a warm heat pad that will help ease the aches. You can also check with your doctor in case you are suffering from cracked nipples or sore nipples.

Doctors Appointment

Once you have been discharged from the hospital and you reach home along with your baby you need to make sure that you keep up with your appointments with your doctor regularly. Apart from helping you physically cope with the stress of a C-section; your doctor will also help you cope with the emotional stress. The doctor also needs to check the wound and see if it is time to take out the stitches or if it needs to be left longer. You need to also inform your doctor if you are experiencing any kind of pain or occasional fever.

Ease Your Fatigue

Fatigue plays an important factor even post-delivery, and just like you did during your pregnancy, you need to make sure that you eat regularly throughout the day so that you will be able to recover from your fatigue and take care of your baby. Eat multiple small meals through the day rather than eating three large meals. Also, try and intake as many proteins and carbs as possible and drink a lot of water. Also keep in mind that just because you have delivered, it doesn't mean that you can consume caffeine or drink alcohol. Try and stay away from this as much as possible because it will affect your mood and it will make it very difficult for you to sleep.

Move Around

While exercises are off limits, you need to make sure that you move around a little bit as this will help you recover from your c-section a lot better. Some women even try and use a stroller to walk around as it helps with their pelvic movements and it also eases the pain. Do not overdo it if it is hurting too much or if you are bleeding. You may want to consult your doctor if moving around the house is extremely difficult.

Chapter 13:
Losing the Weight After Birth

You are expected to gain a certain amount of weight when you are pregnant, and a healthy amount is anywhere between 12 to 16 kgs. Some pregnant women, however, start gaining a lot more than that and while they do lose weight at the delivery table itself, it is important for you to follow a healthy lifestyle if you want to lose more of it. Most of the weight that you gain consists of your actual baby, the placenta, amniotic fluid and breast tissue that starts storing more fat.

If you have gained anywhere above 16 kg, then it's time for you to think about following a healthy diet if you want to shed your pregnancy weight. Most pregnant women tend to gain a lot of weight, and this increases the risk of them becoming overweight post pregnancy and increases the risk of diabetes and heart diseases. It also increases the risk in your future pregnancies. If you want to stay healthy here are a few ways you can get rid of excess weight once you deliver your baby.

Be Realistic

It's easy to look at pictures prior to pregnancy and wish you got back to the same size almost instantly. This is something that doesn't happen soon, and you got to give your body time to heal. It took nine months to get here and it will take you at least the same amount of time if not longer to get back to your pre-pregnancy figure. While this is not impossible to achieve, you must target what's important to make sure you give yourself a realistic time frame, so you don't disappoint yourself. You should try to lose about 1 kg or 2 kgs in a month and nothing more because anything higher than this means you are not losing weight in a healthy way and this will affect the growth and management of your baby's weight too.

Don't Crash Diet

This diet is not recommended for new moms because it doesn't focus on nutrient content. Your body will not be able to provide the right nourishment for your baby if you are breastfeeding. A crash diet simply means to cut down on your meals and eat very small proportions without taking into consideration the kind of nutrition you're providing to your body. While this diet worked when you were a teenager, it's not healthy for you to go on a crash diet when you're a mom because you need to keep yourself strong and nourished if you want to look after your baby and keep your baby healthy. You should plan effective long-term solutions to lose weight where your health is kept at a top priority. Opting in for weight loss diets that do not provide your body with effective nutrition will decrease the amount of breast milk your body forms and your baby will be left hungry and malnourished.

Breastfeed If You Can

Nowadays several doctors recommend formula milk because women want to get back to work as soon as possible and it's difficult for them to breastfeed their babies. If you want your baby to stay healthy then breastfeeding is the best solution because it provides complete nutrition that a baby needs for the first six months of life.

Breast milk is vital for the development of a child because it provides a baby with the necessary nutrients and helps the baby's immune system get stronger to fight virus and bacteria.

Wondering how this is related to your health? Did you know that breastfeeding can help reduce the size of the uterus and bring it back to the normal size after birth? Breastfeeding a baby lowers the risk of various problems including diabetes, leukemia, skin conditions and sudden infant death syndrome amongst others.

Women who breastfeed also stay healthy and are less likely to suffer from diabetes, ovarian cancer, breast cancer as well as postpartum depression. If this wasn't enough, breastfeeding also aids in weight loss and women who tend to breastfeed their babies for longer lose more weight in the long run and go back to their pre-pregnancy weight more comfortably.

Count Your Calories

I highly recommend you keep a tab on the kind of food you eat and make sure you know how many calories you are consuming. When it comes to calorie intake, a woman who breastfeeds needs to consume more calories in comparison to one who doesn't. Make sure you check with your doctor or dietitian to see how many calories you can consume. Nowadays you can download a variety of apps on your phone to keep track of your calories, and this helps you to choose a healthy lifestyle and cut down on larger meals to aid in healthy weight loss.

High Fiber Food

Post pregnancy your metabolism rates tend to drop a little which may add to the weight gain. Include high fiber in your meals since these foods not only help with digestion but also accelerate metabolism ensuring you lose weight faster. Fiber helps to keep your system clean and you also tend to eat smaller meals because fiber makes you feel fuller faster.

Choose to Eat Healthy Protein

Not only does protein make you stronger, but it also helps to keep you full and boosts your metabolism aiding in effective weight loss. Amongst healthy proteins, you should try to include as much of eggs and fish, dairy and lean meats in your diet as possible.

Stock Up on Healthy Snacks

The root cause of weight gain in eating unhealthy foods and you only way you will be able to eat this kind of food is when it's in your house. Each time you make a trip to the grocery store make sure you avoid buying unhealthy snacks and opt-in for healthy alternatives to munch on every time you feel hungry.

Avoid Processed Foods

Processed foods are very high and unhealthy fats along with sugar, calories, and salt. When you consume processed foods daily, your weight loss efforts will go in vain. Some of the fast foods you should avoid pre-packed cookies, chips, candies, ready mixes, and ready meals. Processed foods also contribute to eating disorders and can cause a lot of health complications for you. The best thing to do is to replace processed foods with nutrient-rich foods and start your weight loss journey on a healthy note.

Stop Consuming Alcohol

While alcohol in small quantities, such as red wine, does have certain health benefits, you need to make sure you stay away from alcohol if you want to lose weight. Alcohol is usually packed with a lot of calories and does not provide any kind of nutrition to your body.

Alcohol also causes a condition where the fat gets stored around the organs causing a belly fat. The worst part about alcohol is that it can cause a reduction in the volume of breast milk and very small amounts of alcohol can also be passed on to a baby through breast milk.

If you would like to drink regularly and you're breastfeeding a baby, you need to make sure you leave an enough gap between drinking and feeding your baby, so the alcohol is out of your body and not passed onto your baby. As a rule of thumb, you should wait at least 2 hours before you breastfeed your baby after drinking alcohol.

Exercising Helps

Exercising is not only helpful during your pregnancy, but it also helps to improve your health and lose weight after delivering a baby. There are various cardio exercises such as jogging, walking, interval training, cycling and running that will help you burn a lot of calories. These exercises also help to improve the health of your heart, and it reduces the risk of diabetes. However, you should know that just by exercising you will not be able to lose weight. '

You need to combine exercise with a good nutritional diet to help burn fat quickly. The combination of exercising and dieting is something you need to adapt to when looking to lose weight post-delivery. If you have had a C-section, you need to check with your doctor regarding the time to wait before you start exercising. You need to give your stomach and the pelvic area enough time to heal as rushing into exercising may cause health complications.

Resistance Training

Resistance training can help you lose weight and retain your muscle mass. When you combine resistance training along with a healthy diet, you will be able to lose weight effectively and improve your heart health. It goes without saying that you need approval from your doctor before you start weight training because your body has gone through a lot of stress and you may want to go easy a little bit. Another problem that comes with weight training is you will not find time to exercise when there is a baby that you must handle. You can try watching videos online or downloading mobile apps that will help you exercise while you are at home rather than heading out to a gym.

Drinking Water

Water is essential when it comes to staying healthy as well as losing weight. Staying hydrated is extremely important when you are breastfeeding your baby, and this is the reason you need to continue drinking water on a regular basis. Drinking enough water will also help reduce your calorie intake and it can reduce your appetite as well. Try to drink at least two liters of water daily as it can help with your weight loss and keep you hydrated. If you are exercising along with breastfeeding, then you may need to drink more water.

Get Sufficient Sleep

Sleep deprivation can affect your weight negatively. While getting sleep with a newborn child at home is extremely difficult, you should make sure that you sleep at every chance you get. You need to make sure that you are using the help of your partner as well as family members and friends so that you may be able to sleep while they take care of your baby.

Support Group

There are several support groups to help women with weight loss. When you join a support group, you will be able to stay motivated to achieve weight loss goals, and this will also ensure you get advice from other women who are on the same journey as you. Only women who have dealt with pregnancy will be able to understand the pain of another woman and this is where a support group comes in handy.

Asking Others for Help

You should never hesitate when it comes to asking your family members or friends for help. Several women usually go into depression because they do not have anyone around to help them and this can have a very negative impact on the baby as well. Your friends or family members can help with running errands or helping around the house. Some of them can even help take you to the doctor or your dietician, and this will go a long way in helping you with your weight loss process.

Avoid Consuming Sugar

Consuming sugar in the form of fruit juices or sugary drinks add a lot of calories and do not really provide nutrition to your body. You should also stay away from refined carbs so that you do not increase the risk of heart diseases and diabetes. Cutting down on added sugar will help you lose weight quickly, and it will also make your body healthier.

Chapter 14:
Newborn Must Haves

Pregnancy is tough and stressful, and your first pregnancy is usually going to be the most difficult because you don't really know what you should and shouldn't buy.

While it's essential for you to have a clear list of what's important, you should also understand unnecessary expenses and avoid them. I've discussed what needs to be avoided in the next chapter, and this one focuses on everything you need for your newborn baby. These are the kind of things you can add to your gift registry to cut down on your expenses and make sure you get the stuff you need.

Baby Diapers

You can never have enough diapers because babies need a lot of them and they go through at least five to seven changes a day and sometimes more, which means a pack of 50 diapers won't even last a week. There are some amazing baby infant diapers that you can invest in or add to your gift registry, so you are prepared when your baby poops. Make sure to select one that is designed for infant skin because an infant has very sensitive skin and using a diaper that is not designed for an infant could cause rash and infection.

Baby Wipes

Baby wipes are just as important as diapers because when you change your baby diapers you need something to clean up your baby and using cloth or cotton isn't recommended. If you are adding wipes to your gift registry, try registering for a bulk packet because these don't go bad for a long time and they will last you a couple of months. There are different kinds of baby wipes available so look for something that is soothing and designed for sensitive baby skin.

Diaper Rash Cream or Ointment

No matter how careful you are, your baby will end up with rashes on their bottom, and the best way to treat this rash or sore skin is to use a good quality baby rash cream or ointment. Always consult with your pediatrician to figure out which ointment or cream is good for your baby. You need to look for something that's not chemical based and has all organic natural materials, so it is safe on your baby's bottom.

Burp Cloth

It is highly recommended you invest in a ton of burp cloths because your baby is more likely to make a mess during the first three months and you should always be ready to clean up later. This cloth usually comes in a bundle of either 3 or 6 so add about two or three bundles to your gift registry just to keep some extra handy.

Feeding Bottles and Storage Bags

A lot of women need to get back to work soon after they have had a baby and, in such situations, you either need to pump milk out of the breast and store it in a bottle/bag or prepare formula for your baby. Irrespective of which route you take; you will need a lot of bottles and breast milk bags to store the milk. Try adding at least half a dozen bottles and bags to the list, so you have enough time to sterilize them before you use them.

Quick tip - Make sure you sterilize the bag and the bottle before you store milk in it because newborns are very sensitive, and the stomach cannot handle anything out of the ordinary.

Rubbing Alcohol and Cotton Swabs

Once you bring your baby back home from the hospital, you need to clean the umbilical cord. For you to do this, you must use rubbing alcohol and cotton swabs. This is something not a lot of people will tell you about, and most mothers are not even prepared about what needs to be done for them to clean the umbilical cord regularly. Make sure to ask a midwife or the doctor to teach you the correct method of cleaning the cord, so you don't hurt your baby.

First Aid Kit

A first aid kit should be at the top of your priority list even before your baby is born. I didn't realize this until later when my husband panicked and ran out the door to the nearest pharmacy to get one. Your first aid kit should have a nose sucker, thermometer and basic medications your doctor has recommended for your baby.

Nail Clippers

While we're about a first aid kit, I'd like to talk about the importance of nail clippers specifically designed for infants. Cutting the nails of a baby is so underrated, and parents usually believe they can use any nail clippers, but this is not the case. I didn't realize the importance of a nail clipper until I had scratch marks all over my breasts because it's my baby's long nails and my inability to cut them with an adult nail clipper. There are safe to use baby nail clippers available that you can safely cut your baby's nails with. I highly recommend getting one of these.

Baby Formula

If you plan on getting back to work in a few weeks post-delivery, you need to consider getting your baby used to the formula because you will not manage to pump out a lot of milk and store it in order to feed your baby throughout the day. While breastmilk is ideally recommended for the first six months, if you can't give your baby breastmilk you can always alternate between formula and breastmilk depending on how hectic your schedule is.

Pacifiers

Most babies need a pacifier to keep them calm and help them feel secure when they're not breastfeeding. If you plan on getting your baby a pacifier, look for soft pacifiers that won't hurt your babies' gums. Try investing in a couple of them so that you can keep sterilizing and cleaning them from time to time.

Breast Pump

I can't stress enough on how effective this pump was when I got back to work. While it is a personal choice, you can always try getting on manual one that doesn't cost so much and see whether it works well for you or not. The benefit of using a breast pump is that your baby is not dependent on you and you have a little freedom and time where you could just go relax and rejuvenate yourself.

Baby Lotion

Baby lotion is essential to ensure that the baby does not suffer from dry skin or any kind of rashes after having a bath. It is essential to make sure that your baby is comfortable once he or she has had a bath and al lotion will help soothe the skin from outside and keep it moist from within.

Wash Cloths

You need to have a few washcloths in hand when you have a baby around. It is important to know that your baby will drool most of the time and there will be a lot of wiping that you will need to do around the mouth and the chest area. It is best not using a towel because a towel may cause irritation to the baby's skin and this is where a washcloth will come very handy.

Baby Shampoo

You need to take care of your baby's hair from the first month itself. Apart from investing and lotions you also need to make sure you invest in the best baby shampoo that will help treat your baby's hair with care. There are several no-tear baby shampoo brands you can consider. You won't need to purchase a very big bottle because you need to use a very tiny drop each time you bathe your baby.

Baby Bathtub

Many people use the adult bathtub to bathe their baby. It is important you purchase a baby bathtub, so your baby has his or her own space when they are having a bath. A baby bathtub is not slippery, and it is safe for babies to use. Adult bathtubs, on the other hand, can be slippery and if your baby has the habit of standing up while having a bath, this could cause accidents and unwanted injuries which could be avoided with the baby bathtub.

Crib Along with Mattress

Getting a crib for your baby is essential and you can also ensure that you get a crib that will match the decor of the baby room. While purchasing a crib, you also need to make sure you invest in a top-quality mattress that will keep your baby very comfortable. The reason you need to purchase a baby mattress is because you would not want a baby to sleep on anything that could irritate his or her skin.

Bed Linens

Newborns are extremely messy when it comes to pooping or even throwing up after eating. While it is not advisable to feed a baby in the crib, if you must do that, you need to make sure you invest in a good set of bed linens. It is always good to invest in three or four sets of linens so that you can keep swapping them as and when the baby dirties one of them.

Blankets

Swaddling a newborn baby is essential, and therefore you need to purchase blankets that will help the baby feel extremely secure and warm. Newborn babies need to be wrapped tightly because they are used to being snug in the womb. This is where a swaddling blanket comes extremely handy. If your baby is not very comfortable with being swaddled, then you can leave one hand outside the blanket, and the baby will think that he or she is not wrapped.

Clothes for Your Baby

You need to invest in a lot of onesies and gowns that will make it easy for you to change the diaper for your baby. Most of the clothes for babies these days are available with the button at the bottom that will allow you to change the diaper very easily without having to take out the top. Clothes are available in various sizes but always make sure that you invest in something that would fit a 3-month-old because your baby would grow very fast, and there is no point purchasing new clothes every month.

Socks

A newborn needs socks all the time. Although one may feel that they do not really need to cover their baby's feet in summer, it is important because your baby's skin is very sensitive, and you would not want to expose the skin to the elements. This is the reason you also need to purchase a hat that will come handy during the summer as well as the winter.

Car Seat

A car seat is the most important item that you need to purchase for your baby. You should always purchase a new car seat as opposed to purchasing a used car seat because the used car seat may not be able to withstand a crash. The installation of the car seat must be done properly. Look for a car seat that has excellent safety ratings.

Stroller

It is important to have a stroller; however, you can always combine a stroller along with the car seat that you purchase. There are several brands that offer this combination; however, you need to check the safety aspect of the seat before you go ahead and get excited about the combo offer.

Diaper Bags

Catherine Emily

This is something that you will have to purchase irrespective of how old your baby is. When you move around with your baby outside the house, you will want to carry extra diapers along with creams as well as baby wipes. Always look for a diaper bag that has an insulated section that will help keep bottles cold or warm as per your food requirements.

Chapter 15:
Don't Fall for These Money Traps

Every parent wants to give their baby the best, and there's nothing wrong with this. However, you need to learn to draw a line between what's necessary for your baby and what is an unnecessary expense. There are going to be a lot of new parents who will come and advise you with regards to baby products that they believe are must-haves. Here are a few of these things I believe are a complete waste of money and should be avoided.

Baby Wipe Warmer

I never really understood the concept of a baby wipe warmer because you don't have to wipe your baby's bottom with a warm wipe since cold ones are always preferred. Warm wipes could cause a little irritation on your baby's skin, and unless you are storing your wipes in the freezer, you won't need this warmer. If it is cold in the city you live in, just warm a little water and dip the wipe inside the water before using it on your baby. It's economical and makes a lot of sense.

Baby Seat

A baby seat is something you need to avoid, and while it has become a popular item to have in a household, it is best avoided. It is dangerous forcing your baby to sit even before they are ready to walk, and this could cause a major accident. When your baby becomes ready to sit just use a normal chair!

Talcum Powder

Baby talcum powder has been popular, and people are so used to patting the baby's bottoms with this powder every time they have a bath. However, this is best avoided because there have been reports of baby talcum powder being linked to ovarian cancer.

Baby Food Blender

A baby blender works just as effectively as your blender, and it does nothing different. You can blend your baby's food in your regular blender and investing in a baby blender makes no sense.

Expensive Swings and Rockers

Most new parents get frustrated when their baby does not sleep because they need to be held all the time. One of the things that most parents do is invest in expenses swings or rockers that they feel will put the baby to sleep. What these parents don't realize is the child will eventually start sleeping on their own, and the rocker will just be a waste of money lying in the corner of the room. As parents, you should take turns to hold the baby because this phase is not going to last long, and babies outgrow it very quickly.

Emergency Bottle and Formula

When you are not breastfeeding, it is always advisable to purchase formula because it will help provide nourishment to the baby. However, if you are breastfeeding and you do not have to feed anything else to the baby there is no point in purchasing formula just for the heck of it. Having formula around could even be a barrier to you breastfeeding your baby and this is the reason you need to keep it away for as long as possible when you are breastfeeding your baby.

Baby Shoes

These are a complete no-no. Your baby is not going to walk until he or she is about 7 to 8 months old. There is no point in purchasing shoes for a 1 month or 2-month-old baby because it is never going to be used. There are parents who spend hundreds of dollars on expensive branded shoes just because they want their baby to look good. Making such investments is of no use until your baby starts walking.

Baby Walkers

Let me make one thing straight - a walker will not teach your baby to walk. Most babies can figure out walking on their own. We should all remember that our parents learned to work even when walkers were not even invented. Some babies learn to work later than other babies; however, this should not be a cause for concern. Forcing your baby to walk with the assistance of a walker is not recommended.

Hooded Towels

Babies need towels however; they do not need towels that come with a hood. Babies grow at a very fast pace in the first year and purchasing a towel with the tiny little hood will be of no use in a couple of weeks.

Pregnancy is a long and beautiful journey that has its ups and downs. While you can try to figure out a few hacks to help you through your journey, you also need to remind yourself that every individual is different and what works well for someone else may not work as effectively for you. Take time to figure out your rhythm, and you'll get better with each day.

The journey of parenting begins from conception, and it's a role you need to live up to, every day of your life. While you'll enjoy it for the most part, for the times you don't - just take a deep breath and start over! It's not about perfection, but about enjoying parenthood and making the most of it.

If you find this book helpful in anyway a review to support my endeavors is much appreciated.

Mindful Pregnancy for New Moms

www.ingramcontent.com/pod-product-compliance
Lightning Source LLC
Chambersburg PA
CBHW020359080526
44584CB00014B/1094